STAFF DEVELOPMENT GUIDE
PRIMARY
K-2

HARCOURT BRACE & COMPANY

Orlando   Atlanta   Austin   Boston   San Francisco   Chicago   Dallas   New York
Toronto   London

Printed in the United States of America

ISBN 0-15-307431-0

4 5 6 7 8 9 10   082   2000 99 98 97

CONTENTS

You're Invited

Please come to a celebration of your literacy.

When: From ages five to eight

Where: In classrooms near you

Hosts: Teachers everywhere

Events: Storytime, Shared Reading and Writing, Book Talks, Dramatic Enactments, Self-Selected Writing, Independent Reading, Puppetry, Investigations, Reports, Expert Guidance with "the Literacy Puzzle," and More.

To teach reading and writing
in primary classrooms
is to send invitations
that can't be turned down.

"Yes, I'll come."

Invitations expectant
line the shelves
in best jackets,
waiting to dance.

"Yes, I'll be there."

Invitations abundant
in centers and baskets,
on charts
and on rugs.

"I can't wait."

Dr. Nancy Roser

Professor,
Language and
Literacy Studies,
University of Texas
at Austin

Invitations go singing
the language of authors,
the song of the sirens,
creating the lure.

"I must know."

Invitations extended
make each reader welcome,
each writer awaited.

"It won't happen without me."

Invitations repeated,
cast daily and deeply—
received and
accepted.

"I am there."

TEACHER INVENTORY

How Am I Doing?

by **Dr. W. Dorsey Hammond**
Professor of Education, Oakland University,
Rochester, Michigan

Competent professionals are always analyzing their own behaviors. Below are ten teacher behaviors. From time to time, you may want to refer to this list to assess your own strengths.

1 = I need to work on this.
3 = I'm getting better at this behavior.
5 = I feel I do this quite well.

	1	3	5
	Seldom	**Sometimes**	**Always When Appropriate**
1 I read to and share books with my children every day.	1	3	5
2 I use good comprehension strategies such as K-W-L across the curriculum.	1	3	5
3 I give children opportunities to discuss orally what they have read.	1	3	5
4 I encourage children to set their own purposes for reading by using prediction strategies.	1	3	5
5 I am sensitive to wait time, allowing children to self-correct before I intervene.	1	3	5
6 I talk to children about what good readers do: they read for meaning, they have a purpose, they sometimes reread and use look-back strategies, they predict, and they are always trying to make sense.	1	3	5
7 Children in my classroom know they must do their very best, but I am tolerant of their errors when they take risks.	1	3	5
8 I do a lot of modeling in my classroom. For example, sometimes I model my own thinking when I read and when I write and revise.	1	3	5
9 I ask high-level questions that force children to analyze and interpret, not just remember facts.	1	3	5
10 Our classroom is filled with a variety of reading material, including lists, fiction and nonfiction, chapter books, poetry, magazines, and posters.	1	3	5

Harcourt Brace School Publishers

The K–2
Learner

"**T**here are countless opportunities to use print in ways that help children see its value in their lives."

→ Dr. Dorothy Strickland

DEVELOPMENTALLY APPROPRIATE PRACTICE

by Judy Giglio
Educational Consultant and Writer

"A truly appropriate curriculum will not look the same from one classroom of children to the next nor from one year to the next."

Deborah J. Cassidy
and Camille Lancaster
Young Children
Volume 48 Number 6
September 1993

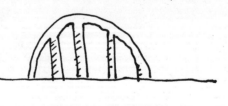

Harcourt Brace School Publishers

Developmentally appropriate practice can be broken down into three parts: activities, materials, and expectations. The activities a teacher plans, the classroom materials he or she provides, and the expectations he or she has for the children—these three elements work together to determine whether a classroom is developmentally appropriate for the children inside it. Which of the classrooms described below sounds more appropriate for children in the primary grades?

Classroom 1

In this classroom, learning centers take up most of the space. Children are involved with small-group, partner, and independent activities as they explore the theme *Community Workers*. A painted mural of workers decorates one wall. Worker mobiles hang from the ceiling. The teacher is working with a small group, while the other children are exploring aspects of the theme in several different learning centers. Two children inspect the homemade calendar to check dates for the visit of the mayor and a class trip to the bakery.

Classroom 2

The children are seated in rows of desks and seem to be attentive to their teacher, who is telling the whole group about community workers. A commercially made bulletin board shows different jobs. Following the lesson, the class discusses the topic during a question-and-answer session led by the teacher. Worksheets are then given to children to complete independently. If they finish their worksheets in time, they will be able to visit the learning centers. The teacher is now seated at her desk, grading papers while keeping a watchful eye on the children.

The task of providing a child-centered classroom and curriculum for a group of highly diverse learners is a challenging one. By definition, developmentally appropriate practice provides for the individual needs and learning styles of *every* child! Add to this the pressures placed on many primary-grade teachers to implement more formal instruction in academic skills.

Yet the teacher in classroom 1 is making it work. How? The chart on page 12 offers some practical insights and suggestions for making any primary classroom more developmentally appropriate.

	What Children Require	Appropriate Practices	Practical Examples of Appropriate Practices
PHYSICAL DEVELOPMENT	Ample space and opportunities for constructive use of energy	Learning centers define the classroom. Children are free to move about. Varied activities are offered.	Provide a variety of centers in which materials evolve with children's changing interests. Children themselves are responsible in large part for managing how they use the centers, how they move from one center to another, and so on. Tables and rugs instead of individual desks allow children to work together or alone.
SOCIAL-EMOTIONAL DEVELOPMENT	Individual recognition	Children have daily opportunities for sharing personal experiences and interests. Individual learning styles are valued. A variety of group patterns are used.	Time for sharing is built into most activities. Progress is assessed through "kid watching," portfolio reviews, and conferences that allow children to take responsibility for their own learning.
COGNITIVE DEVELOPMENT	Opportunities to explore, create, and interact	Provide "generic" learning materials with the greatest possible flexibility. Provide opportunities for practical applications of recently acquired concepts, strategies, and skills.	Plan the curriculum around themes of interest to children. Integrate all curriculum areas around these themes. Invite children to share personal insights and experiences. Explore every theme through literature, music, movement, dramatics, and hands-on activities.
	Integrated, multisensory learning	As much as possible, let the themes drive curriculum in your "core" curriculum areas. Provide for hands-on learning activities. Work with children toward shared goals.	Plan a single open-ended project for each theme. The project should be broad enough that children with diverse interests can contribute in meaningful ways—through art, music, math, science, cooking, dramatics, and so on.

Harcourt Brace School Publishers

CREATING A PRINT-RICH ENVIRONMENT

by Dr. Dorothy S. Strickland

State of New Jersey Professor of Reading, Rutgers University

Surround kindergarten children with print and see how quickly they begin to use it for their own purposes. Include more print in first and second graders' daily activities and see how their literacy is enhanced. Print can be part of virtually any activity—indoors or out, fun or academic, first thing in the morning or just before going home. There are countless opportunities to use print in ways that help children see its value in their lives.

Harcourt Brace School Publishers

The K-2 Learner 11

CREATING AND USING

GENERAL HINTS

- Display children's work at their eye level.
- Arrange bookcases and cabinets to serve as dividers.
- Push desks together to facilitate collaborative learning.
- Help children establish general guidelines for working in centers; e.g., "Use quiet voices" or "Ask a friend for help." Periodically review the list with children, and revise it as they become more independent.

LIBRARY OR BOOK CORNER

Be sure to include:

- A variety of quality literature, including nonfiction
- Big books
- Class- and child-authored books
- Books with a range of levels for independent reading
- Pillows, stuffed animals, and other comfort items
- Special displays of recommended titles

CIRCLE OR RUG AREA

(May be combined with book corner)

- Easel for interactive writing and holding big books

LISTENING CENTER

- Multiple copies of stories and poems on tape
- Tape player and headsets

WRITING CENTER

- Variety of paper
- Blank books
- Alphabet chart
- Primary typewriter and computer
- Writing instruments, including pens, markers, and crayons
- Stapler, glue, and so on
- Display and storage areas for work folders, completed projects, and file boxes
- Chart with names of all class members
- List of frequently used words (word wall)
- Beginning dictionaries

CONTENT-AREA CENTERS

- Informational and story books related to the topic
- Concrete objects related to the topic
- Task cards with suggested activities

ART/MUSIC/DRAMA CENTERS

- Labels for storage boxes for all materials
- Fine-art prints and illustrated songbooks
- Rebus directions for daily activity or exploration

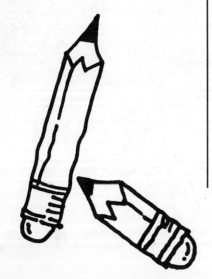

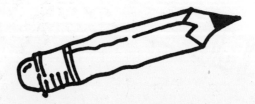

CENTERS EFFECTIVELY

Setting Conditions for Sharing Print in the Classroom

1 Children have access to an abundance of books in their classroom, the school library, and the public library. A plentiful and accessible supply of literary resources is essential to a literature-based language arts program.

2 Time is set aside daily for independent reading in school. For children to view their selection and voluntary reading of books as an important part of their lives, these activities are not relegated to something to be done when they complete their other (and seemingly more important) work or as a homework assignment.

3 Reading aloud to children from various types of literature is a regular part of the language arts program.

4 There is a conscious effort to relate reading and writing instruction. Lessons during writing workshops feature examples from literature: how authors develop a plot, use interesting language, and create good leads and closings. Discussions of this type during reading help children learn to read like a writer.

5 At times, several activities focus on a single work of literature, a particular genre, or the work of a certain author or illustrator. Children need to explore literature in depth to extend their sense of story and develop a better appreciation and understanding of a body of literary work.

6 Finally, children use varied means to respond to literature. Responses may be written or oral, formal or informal. Children have opportunities to respond and share as they read as well as after they finish a book.

25 WAYS TO ADD PRINT TO YOUR CLASSROOM

For this article, we have chosen an assortment of 25 tried-and-true suggestions for adding print to your classroom. Use these ideas as presented, or add your own personal touches to adapt them for your young readers. The end result will be a classroom setting that is rich in print to stimulate daily learning across the curriculum.

1. Word Webs

2. Daily Class Diary

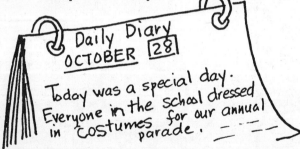

3. Labels

4. Daily Routine Chart

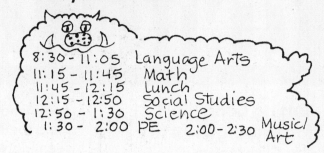

5. Helper Chart

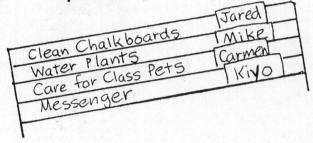

6. News Bulletin Board

7. Thematic Calendar

Harcourt Brace School Publishers

8. Daily Weather Chart

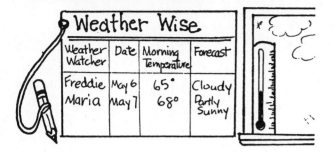

9. Experience Chart

We listened to "The Three Billy-Goats Gruff."
Then we made masks and had a play.
We invited the kindergarten class. We wanted
to learn more about goats so we went to a
farm and saw how goats are milked.
The farmer gave us goat cheese to eat.
Some of us did not like it. We drew
pictures about what we learned.

10. Theme-Related Word Bank

	BIRDS	MAMMALS	INSECTS	REPTILES
A	ant bird	anteater	ant	
N	nuthatch			alligator
I		impala		
M	mallard	moose	moth	iguana
A		armadillo		
L	lark	leopard		
S	sparrow	skunk	ladybug	lizard snake

11. Poem-a-Week Poster

QUESTION

Do you love me?
Or do you not?
You told me once
But I forgot.

Anonymous

12. Our Very Own Word Files

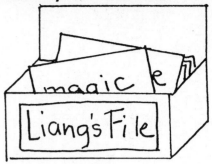

13. Message Center

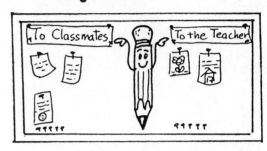

To Classmates   To the Teacher

14. Task Cards

NUMBER SENTENCES   MATH
Look at each picture. Write a number sentence.

Draw a picture for these number sentences.
5+8 = 13   10 - 6 = 4

15. Science Log

Bird-watching Log

Birdwatcher	Date	Bird	Color	Actions
Jason	May 3	robin	brown	hopping and standing
Maria	May 4	wren	brown	sitting in a tree chirping

16. Graphs of All Kinds

Favorite Ways to Eat Apples	
slices	🍎🍎🍎
applesauce	🍎🍎🍎🍎🍎 🍎
apple pie	🍎 🍎🍎🍎
apple juice	🍎 🍎🍎🍎🍎

17. Favorite "Book" Recipes

18. K-W-L Charts

What We Know About Frogs	What We Want to Know About Frogs	What We Learned About Frogs
small green long tongues eat insects hatch from eggs	Are frogs and toads the same? Where do frogs live in winter? Who are their enemies?	

19. Class Lists

Things to do to get ready for Kwanzaa

Who will bring?
ears of corn- J.P. D.W.
straw mat- K.L.
1 black candle- M.P.
3 red candles- S.R.
3 green candles- W.N.

Who will make?
cupcakes- S.T. R.F. M.N.
posters- J.T. C.G. S.G.

20. Birthday Chart

21. Evaluation Charts

Learning Center Report Card		
Report Card for: Native American Center		
Student	Activity You Did	What did you think?
Karl	Totem Poles	I liked making my own totem pole. I put an eagle on top.
Jenny	Sand art	Sand art is pretty but my glue ran all over.

22. Personal Journals

23. Steps in a Process

POTTING PUMPKIN SEEDS
You need: cup   stick
1. Write your name on the stick.
2. Put ½ cup soil in your cup.
3. Put 4 seeds in.
4. Cover the seeds with soil.
5. Put your stick in the cup. Your name should show.
6. Water the seeds.

24. Sign-Up Sheets

OCTOBER 28 is POTATO DAY
What is your favorite way to eat potatoes?

Shane- french fries
Kevin- mashed
Johanna- potato pancakes

25. Estimation Games

How Many?
Larry- 25
Jake- 55
Wen- 47
Pedro- 50

Harcourt Brace School Publishers

Emergent Literacy

"Children know much more about print at an earlier age than we gave them credit for in the past."

→ Patricia Smith

PHONEMIC AWARENESS

by Dr. Hallie Kay Yopp, Professor

Department of Elementary and Bilingual Education

California State University, Fullerton

Children for whom learning to read is a positive, successful endeavor are often those from print-rich and language-rich environments. They are children who are surrounded by books and other sources of print, who are read to frequently, and who are provided with many opportunities to engage in oral language play.

The importance of oral language play has recently become an area of considerable interest to teachers and researchers. We know from observations of preschoolers that young children have a natural propensity to experiment with sounds. They sing nonsense songs, make up rhymes, create silly words, and repeat utterances they find amusing. Over time, most children in an environment where play with sounds is stimulated will develop **phonemic awareness**—the awareness that their speech is made up of a series of sounds that can be manipulated.

Identifying Phonemic Awareness

A phonemically aware child can mentally manipulate spoken sounds. The child knows that the spoken word *cat* has three sounds and can segment the word to say each sound /k/-/a/-/t/. A phonemically aware child can also blend together three spoken sounds to form a word: /d/-/o/-/g/ is *dog*.

A few children enter kindergarten with a strong sense of phonemic awareness; however, most children lack this insight. You will find that some children are completely unable to make sense of any phonemic awareness activities, whereas others quickly catch on to some activities. Some children may be able to identify rhymes (a simpler task that is related to more-sophisticated phonemic awareness tasks) but may be unable to segment sounds. Some children may be able to identify the first sound they hear in a word but may be unable to blend together three spoken sounds to form a word. (See the *SIGNATURES Skills Assessment* Teacher's Edition, Grades 1 and 2, for a tool for assessing phonemic awareness.)

Harcourt Brace School Publishers

Phonemic Awareness Is Not Phonics

Phonemic awareness is not the same as skill in phonics. *Phonics* refers to learning the sounds that letters and letter combinations represent and using that knowledge to sound out words. *Phonemic awareness,* on the other hand, is the recognition that speech is made up of a series of sounds (phonemes) that can be manipulated. The ability to use phonics as a means to decode printed words probably depends on a child's understanding that speech is made up of individual sounds—that is, on phonemic awareness. Without phonemic awareness, teaching a child the sounds that letters represent in speech and asking him or her to "sound and blend" letters make little sense.

What the Research Says

The research in phonemic awareness has been called one of this century's great success stories in education and psychology. We have learned that phonemic awareness is a critical insight that must be developed for independence in reading to occur. It is both a potent predictor of success and a powerful determinant of difficulty in reading acquisition, regardless of instructional approach.

Many studies confirm that phonemic awareness is one ability that separates skilled from disabled readers (Yopp, 1995).

Of great importance is the research that shows that providing children with oral activities that focus their attention on the phonemic base of their speech results in substantial gains in phonemic awareness. Further, children who engage in activities that spark phonemic awareness outperform their control-group counterparts in both reading and spelling achievement!

Classroom Activities for Stimulating Phonemic Awareness

Children should be engaged in many activities that stimulate their interest and give them a chance to experiment with sounds. You can draw children's attention to the component sounds of their speech with songs, riddles, games, and shared readings of stories that deal playfully with speech sounds. Keep these activities informal and entertaining to ensure that children will enjoy manipulating and experimenting with their language and will look forward to new, more challenging ways to reflect on and play with language.

Phonemic Awareness Activities That You Can Integrate Throughout the Day

Activities like these will help children focus on the sounds in their spoken language and will build phonemic awareness. The implications for reading and spelling are profound!

Read and reread stories that play with language. Many books, such as *Dr. Seuss's ABC* or J. Gordon's *Six Sleepy Sheep*, make use of alliteration—nearly all words in each sentence begin with the same sound. Books such as Raffi's *Down by the Bay* explicitly deal with rhyming words.

Help children create new songs, using familiar melodies and an alliterative pattern. For "Go In and Out the Window," sing "Oh, silly Sam's sister, oh, silly Sam's sister, Oh, silly Sam's sister is so so silly!" Children will enjoy making up their own versions.

Have children draw out the sounds in familiar poems and rhymes, as in the lines Rrrrrrrround is a pancake. Rrrrrrrround is a plum.

Play guessing games in which you indicate that you are thinking of something (an animal, vehicle, person), and give sounds as clues. "I'm thinking of an animal. The sounds in its name are /b/-/a/-/t/." Children must blend the sounds together in order to identify the animal.

Booklist

Down by the Bay, Raffi (1988).

Dr. Suess's ABC, Dr. Suess (1963).

Six Sleepy Sheep, J. Gordon (1993).

Harcourt Brace School Publishers

SHARED READING

by Dr. Dorothy S. Strickland

"Goodnight, Moon!" Three-year-old Ryan claps his hands and cuddles close to his mom as he yells out a line from one of his favorite books. His mother smiles and reads on, slowing her pace or remaining silent at key points where Ryan joins in "reading" aloud.

For generations, shared reading experiences at home have helped countless youngsters approach beginning reading with joy and ease. In today's classrooms, teachers use this technique to extend the reading development of children who are lucky enough to have been read to at home and to provide a vital literacy experience for those who have not been read to.

What is shared reading?

Shared reading is an interactive process in which teacher and children participate together to read a text. The text may be a big book, a chart, or any other print in the classroom environment. Predictable materials with repetitive pictures, words, and phrases work well. Shared reading can be used from prekindergarten right through the primary grades. The difficulty and complexity of the materials can be increased as children gain confidence and skill.

Repeated readings are key to the success of shared reading. Children need many varied experiences with familiar whole texts. Group discussion, art activities, shared writing, and drama are some of the different ways children might respond to the same text.

Why is shared reading important?

- Students are provided with a model of a skilled, enthusiastic adult reader.
- Group reading is a positive, low-risk literacy experience.
- Instruction is automatically differentiated since all children can function at their own levels.
- Specific skills may be taught as children learn from and enjoy the text.
- Oral language is developed as children read with the group and participate in discussion.

What happens during shared reading?

Shared reading involves a great deal of teacher/child interaction. Most importantly, both teacher and children are ACTIVE.

Roles of Teacher and Child During Shared Reading	
Teacher	**Child**
Presents whole tasks	Experiences whole tasks
Performs with child	Performs with teacher
Gives active support	Gains knowledge
Intervenes when needed	Internalizes textual frameworks and language patterns
Gradually releases support	Internalizes strategies
Offers numerous and varied opportunities to apply what has been learned	Practices strategies, using whole texts in meaningful contexts
Introduces increasingly difficult tasks	

How will I know if children understood the story?

The first time you read a story, try to include the following:

1. A discussion of cover, title, and author
2. Opportunities for prediction
3. Follow-up activities:
   Confirm children's predictions.
   Help children relate the story to their personal experiences. Ask open-ended discussion questions:

   - What was your favorite part?
   - Has something like that ever happened to you?
   - What if _____ hadn't happened in the story?
   - How else could the story have ended?

Why should I reread a story?

A story, poem, or song that is suitable for a shared reading should probably be reread several times, unless, of course, your children did not like it. If the story was first read purely for enjoyment, a lot of learning opportunities are lost if the story is not read at least one more time. Here's just a short list:

1. Increasing participation
2. Exploring conventions of print
3. Extending comprehension
4. Expanding vocabulary
5. Responding creatively; relating to other curriculum areas

Increasing Participation

a. **Choral reading**   With each rereading, more and more children are able to join in and recite more and more of the text, with ever greater accuracy. Repeated readings of a classic like *Brown Bear, Brown Bear, What Do You See?* will illustrate this perfectly. With each rereading, children are attending to picture clues (red bird, purple cat), clues from repetitions built into the text (*what do you see?/looking at me*), and clues from their own understanding of the story. (Animals take turns telling what they see.)

b. **Other ways to join in**   Depending on the story, children can create sound effects, make hand/body movements, or clap to the rhythm of the story line. (See the article on page 41.) The text patterns of some stories lend themselves to special group configurations. For example, when rereading *Brown Bear*, a teacher might have half the class ask the questions and the other half recite the answers.

Harcourt Brace School Publishers

c. Questions and discussion The very first time they hear a story, children want and deserve an uninterrupted reading. The second or third time through, however, there's time to really pick apart the story and to explore elements that intrigue or confuse individual children. During subsequent readings, you and your class can

- ask or answer questions that arise during the reading.
- talk in depth about the pictures.
- let individuals share similar experiences they've had.
- discuss vocabulary.

Exploring Conventions of Print

a. Book awareness For very inexperienced readers, this may be as fundamental as identifying the basic parts of a book and what they are for. It also means knowing where to start reading—in the book and on each page.

b. Words, spaces, letters, punctuation Big books and charts are wonderful tools for minilessons about

- ***words and word spaces*** Frame words with your hands, and talk about how they're separated; have children do the same. Have children count how many times a particular word is repeated on a page or in an entire story. Have children find all the words with the same beginning or ending letters or sounds, all the words that start with the same sound as their first name, and all the words that begin with a capital letter. With a self-stick note, cover a word that you think children will be able to predict. Ask the group to guess the word as you read the page aloud together.

- ***letters*** Frame a word, and talk about the letters in it. How many are there? How many of any single letter? Whose name begins with one of the letters? Which letter or letters stand for the beginning sound you hear when you say the word? Is this g written the same way that *you* write a g? How are the g's different?

- ***sentences, capitalization, and punctuation*** Make phrase and sentence strips for children to find and match with repeated text in the big book. Children can practice reading the words within the story first and then on the sentence strip. Have volunteers find the capital letter that begins each sentence, and talk about this rule. Point out that the word *I* is always written as a capital letter. Talk about different end marks and why they are used with statements, commands, questions, and exclamations.

Extending Comprehension

a. Predicting Even after young children have heard a story several times, they still love to predict what will happen next. You can make this more challenging by asking them to identify picture clues they use, clues from their own experiences, or clues from the structure of the story itself.

b. Sequencing Have volunteers help you make sequencing cards based on events in the story. A story like *Flower Garden* is easy for children to sequence because the events take place in a logical order. Let a group of children work together to hold up the cards in sequence during one shared reading of the story.

c. Finding patterns Have children express in their own words the pattern in a predictable story. Children can also discuss similarities and differences among stories they know: "How is 'Five Little Ducks ' like the song 'Roll Over'?" (One is subtracted each time.)

d. Classifying/Categorizing Have children make lists of people, places, animals, and things that arise naturally from the story. For example, they might make lists of large and small animals; fierce and friendly animals; and no-legged, two-legged, four-legged, and six-legged animals after reading *Who Is the Beast*? Post the lists where children can add to them and use them in their own writing.

Expanding Vocabulary

a. Synonyms With a self-stick note, cover a word that children are likely to know within the context of the story, such as *littlest* or *biggest* in "The Three Billy-Goats Gruff." Ask children to supply other words that mean about the same thing. Write them on the note, and reread that part of the story, using the children's words.

b. Imagery Children can substitute other animals in a story like *Quick as a Cricket*. (quick as a deer; mean as a bee) Make new big books using their ideas and illustrations.

c. Word webs Put on the board an important story word such as *friend* from *My Friends* or *peanut butter* from the jingle "Peanut Butter and Jelly." Have children brainstorm associated words to add to the web. Display the web where children can add to it and can use the words in their writing.

What can I learn from a shared reading?

Most often, shared reading in the classroom is a group experience. It is an excellent opportunity to *observe* the overall progress of the group. Later, when you *analyze* the information from your observations, you have a basis for planning future learning experiences.

During shared readings, you can also focus on the development of specific individuals. An individual might be selected for special monitoring because of one of the following reasons:

1. The child rarely participates in the group. Could he or she have a visual or an auditory problem? Is the problem shyness or limited language development? Is there a distraction that prevents this child from fully participating?

2. The child appears to be functioning at a very advanced level. Could he or she handle more challenging materials? Would this child feel comfortable being a buddy reader with a less-able classmate?

Use the copying master on the next page to help you assess the progress of your group during shared readings throughout the year.

Harcourt Brace School Publishers

Shared Reading Observational Checklist

Child _____ Teacher _____ Grade _____

Concepts About Print *Child demonstrates understanding of the following concepts:*	Date	Date	Date	Date	Date	Date
Print contains meaning						
Pictures convey and enhance meaning						
Left-to-right direction						
Top-to-bottom direction						
Book title						
Author						
Illustrator						
Sentence						
Word						
Letter						
Similarities in words and letters						

Comprehension and Interpretation *Child demonstrates understanding of familiar books and stories through the following behaviors:*	Date	Date	Date	Date	Date	Date
Discusses meanings related to characters and events						
Makes and confirms reasonable predictions						
Infers words in cloze-type activities						
Remembers sequence of events						
Compares/contrasts events within and between books						
States main ideas						
States causes and effects						
Recalls details						

Interest in Books and Reading *Child demonstrates an interest in books and reading through the following behaviors:*	Date	Date	Date	Date	Date	Date
Shows interest in listening to stories						
Participates in reading patterned and predictable language						
Engages in talk about books and stories						
Requests favorite books to be read aloud						
Views himself/herself as a reader						
Voluntarily uses the classroom library						
Shows pleasure in reading independently						

FOR THE LOVE *of* READING

by **Dr. Bernice E. Cullinan**
Professor of Reading, New York University

No child was ever born wanting to learn to read, just as no child is born wanting to play professional football, climb the Himalayas, or become an Olympic ice skater. The adults around them help shape what children want. We call it building motivation, creating a desire, or developing a hunger.

We entice children to learn to read by reading to them—engaging stories, compelling facts, and ridiculous rhymes. If parents have done their job well by reading to children during the preschool years, the children come to school yearning to read. These children understand that reading is worth the effort, that it proceeds from left to right across the page, and that some words begin with the same letter. They are off and running, eager to devour print and to try their hands at creating it.

If, however, children come to school without the basic background knowledge that wonderful things come from books, you need to start there—reading aloud, reading together, singing songs, and saying rhymes as a group. These endeavors not only help children learn how to read but also encourage them to want to read.

The materials you select can help ease children into the reading habit. For example, books with strong repetitive, rhythmic, and rhyming language will help children break the code easily. The words sound the way children think they should and match the sounds children expect to hear. Words that sound alike most often look alike, too; children recognize the similarity in spelling patterns quickly.

Rhyming words, patterned language, and rhythmic texts create what we call "predictable" texts because readers are able to predict what is coming next in the sentence. If you were to say

"Pease porridge hot / Pease porridge cold Pease porridge in the pot / Nine days ...,"

Children would yell out "old!"

If you were to say

"Humpty Dumpty sat on a wall. Humpty Dumpty had a great ..."

Children would say "fall."

If you were to read *Henny Penny*, children would soon join in to say with you, *"Oh, Ducky Lucky! The sky is falling. And we are going to tell the king."*

If you were to read "Five Little Ducks," children would sing and say the traditional rhyme with the group.

"Five little ducks went swimming one day,
Over the hills and far away.
Mother Duck said, 'Quack, quack, quack, quack.'
But only four little ducks came back."

Poetic language tickles the tongue, tingles the mind, and intrigues the ear.

Poetry and verse as predictable texts are easy to read. They contain short lines with few words per line, rhyming words, melody, few words that say a great deal, much white space with few words on a page, and the natural language of childhood.

Harcourt Brace School Publishers

Poetry helps children learn to listen.
Children pay attention to poetry because it accentuates the sounds of language—for example, *"An earthworm doesn't make a sound/ When he's working underground."* (Ernesto Galarza); *"Caterpillars crawl humpity-hump/ Little frogs go jumpity-jump."*; and *"Always quiet,/ Always blinking,/ By day sleeping,/ At night winking."* (Nelly Palacio Jaramillo)

Poetry teaches children new vocabulary. Poetry uses interesting words in interesting ways. Children notice new words and repeat them in their conversations.

Poetry helps children learn to read.
Beginning readers learn to decode print in poetry because the lines are short, the words rhyme, and the accent falls on meaningful words. These clues tell readers what is coming next—for example,

> *"Elephant,*
> *Elephant,*
> *Big as a House!*
> *They tell me*
> *That you*
> *Are afraid of a*
> *Mouse."* (Langston Hughes)

Poetry helps children make connections between letters and sounds.
Children learn phonics when they see patterns of letters and sounds repeated in poetry and verse. Poetry helps reluctant or disabled readers because there are not many words on a page. Poems leave much white space— open space—on a page. The short lines and limited number of words do not intimidate a child learning to read—for example, *"Good books./ Good times./ Good stories./ Good rhymes."* (Lee Bennett Hopkins)

Poetry helps children learn to write.
Children learn to read by writing; poetry lets them in on the secret of how words work. They discover that if they can write *my hat*, they can also write *my cat* and *my bat*. When they learn to write *quack*, they can also write *shack, snack, tack, track,* and *backpack.* These discoveries turn struggling writers into wordsmiths—for example, *"Send*

in the Cat/ to chase that Rat!/ Send in the Hog/ to shoo that Dog!/ Send in the Cow./ Send that Cow NOW!" (Wong Herbert Yee)

Poetry helps children learn to think. It shows them new images and new ways to view the world—for example, *"A dream is just a pillow away."* (from "How Far" by Leland B. Jacobs in *Big Book of Rhymes*); *"I've also proved by actual test,/ A wet dog is the lovingest."* (Ogden Nash); and *"A soft dog,/ A furry dog,/ A call-her-and-she'll-hurry dog."* (Nancy Klima)

Strategies for the Classroom

Copy poems onto large chart paper and laminate for durability. Use the charts to read together and to point out similarities in word patterns, initial consonants, and other phonics elements.

Read the same poems over and over until children know them by heart. Present a program for other class groups or for parents to demonstrate children's wealth of poetic knowledge.

Create a display that includes poems children love and poems children write. On a table, bulletin board, or wall, display poems children have brought in, written, or copied from books.

B O O K L I S T

Eek! There's a Mouse in the House, by Wong Herbert Yee, Houghton Mifflin, 1992.

Grandmother's Nursery Rhymes, by Nelly Palacio Jaramillo, Henry Holt, 1994.

Kids Pick the Funniest Poems, compiled by Bruce Lansky, Meadowbrook Press, 1991.

Questions, selected by Lee Bennett Hopkins, HarperCollins, 1992.

The Sweet and Sour Animal Book, by Langston Hughes, Oxford University Press, 1994.

WHEN A FEATHER FALLS:
USING POETRY WITH YOUNG CHILDREN

BY DR. LEE BENNETT HOPKINS

Poet, Author, Anthologist

"Pueblo Reflections," a poem in the award-winning
book *Spirit Walker* by Nancy Wood (Doubleday, 1993) begins

> **66** When a feather falls at your feet, it means
>
> you are to travel on wings of curiosity. **99**

When I started my career as an elementary school teacher in 1960, the feather that fell at my feet was one that quivered with poetry. I quickly realized how poetry could change and enhance the lives of my children, how it could stir their emotions with a minimum of words and lines like no other form of literature. Via poetry, my children and I could laugh and cry, sing and shout, be totally surprised and awed at what poetry could give us.

Throughout my entire professional life, I have continued to use poetry with children on every grade level, at every age, from preschoolers through college-schoolers!

Let the feather fall at your feet, and your teaching life will be enhanced, too.

Use poetry every day in every area of the curriculum.

Think about combining other works of fiction and nonfiction with poetry, no matter what the topic is. You will find there are poems written on almost any subject—from fingerprints to wildflowers, secrets to seals, dreamers to dancers. Anthologies can provide a wealth of synchronizing selections centered around powerful themes and topics. Many such groupings can help you connect literature to science, social studies, and math.

Start children on a search for poetry. If children enjoy a particular poet's work, encourage them to seek out individual collections or verses the poet has written that appear in anthologies. Chances are if children delight in a poem by John Ciardi, Eve Merriam, or Nikki Giovanni, for example, they will appreciate other offerings by the same poets.

Once poetry becomes a part of children's repertoires, class projects might center around choosing "The Poem of the Week," "The Poet of the Month," or "Best Poems About _____"—any topic of the children's choice.

When the feather falls at your feet, pick it up. See how quickly you and your children will "travel on wings of curiosity."

I know you will.

Happy journeying!

BOOKLIST

Pass the Poetry, Please! by Lee Bennett Hopkins. HarperCollins, 1987.

Let's Do a Poem: Introducing Poetry to Children by Nancy Larrick. Delacorte, 1991.

The Random House Book of Poetry for Children ed. by Jack Prelutsky. Random House, 1983.

Using Poetry Across the Curriculum: A Whole Language Approach by Barbara Chatton. Oryx Press, 1993.

Harcourt Brace School Publishers

Understanding Diversity Through Literature

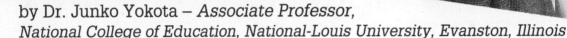

by Dr. Junko Yokota – *Associate Professor,*
National College of Education, National-Louis University, Evanston, Illinois

The role of multicultural literature in the classroom is to provide all students with extensive opportunities to learn about the contributions, achievements, and traditions of people from diverse groups, to see their own culture depicted in literature, and to develop accurate concepts of self, others, and the world around us.

Guidelines for Choosing Multicultural Literature

Literature forms the basis of a truly integrated reading and language arts program. Using *multicultural* literature simply means that children benefit from a rich variety of the best authors, illustrators, characters, and real-life heroes. Here are some guidelines to keep in mind when selecting multicultural literature:

- Include a **variety of genres:** folklore, poetry, historical fiction, informational articles, realistic fiction, biography and autobiography, fantasy, and mystery.
- Select literature that is written and illustrated by someone who holds an **"insider's" perspective** of the culture portrayed.
- Check for **cultural accuracy,** both in the overall treatment of various issues and in the details. (Tip: If you are not sure of the accuracy yourself, ask colleagues and other community members for advice.)
- Try to find literature that is **culturally specific:** a story about Korean Americans rather than Asian Americans or about a Sioux family rather than a Native American family.
- Include literature about ethnic groups in the **United States,** both present and past, suburban, urban, and rural.
- Include literature with settings in other countries.
- Depict **differing perspectives** to show multidimensionality within groups; recognize that there are many differences within as well as between various ethnic and cultural groups.

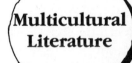

This chart shows one way of thinking about multicultural understanding. If your students can perform on all three of these levels, you will know that you have helped them appreciate diversity.

Levels of Understanding

Multicultural Literature

Achievement Level
Students are aware of the contributions of all groups and cultures in art, science, literature, and other areas.

Diverse Perspectives Level
Students are able to see events and ideas from the viewpoints of people with various backgrounds.

Decision-Making Level
Students draw on their understanding of achievements and perspectives of diverse groups as they make decisions and judgments.

Multicultural Infusion

by Dr. Margaret A. Gallego

Dr. Gallego is Assistant Research Scientist at the University of California, San Diego's Laboratory of Comparative Human Cognition.

A child is a member of several groups—a family, a classroom, a community, a culture. The interactions a child has had within these various groups since birth have helped create a unique individual. In a multicultural curriculum, the study of culture is incorporated into daily classroom activities as much to honor each child's own uniqueness as to learn about others. Since basic outlooks and assumptions are formed very early in life, respect for diversity can and should be an underlying goal for every primary classroom.

A Framework for Developing Cultural Awareness

The best way to understand others is to step into their shoes. For young children this means

- meaningful interactions with high-quality multicultural literature.
- hands-on activities that take into account different learning styles—visual, auditory, and kinesthetic.
- immersion for a period of time in a particular culture.

Many teachers build units of study around related pieces of literature. A unit might be

- an author study.
- an illustrator study.
- a group of stories, songs, and poems from a particular culture.
- a topic from social studies or science that ties together several stories, poems, plays, and so on.

One of the main purposes of a multicultural unit of study is to give all children opportunities to succeed, particularly children whose first language is not English. Building equity into the content is essential when planning a unit. Of course, the activities intended to reach this goal should also enhance the reading, writing, and speaking abilities of *every* child.

Harcourt Brace School Publishers

Start with What's Comfortable for You

Multicultural education takes a variety of forms. Some schools have opted for total immersion. Other schools have established separate learning centers that can take small groups of children at a time. Some programs begin within a single classroom committed to cultural awareness and gradually spread through the school. Whatever your situation, don't be afraid to take the plunge! Here are some simple do's and don'ts for getting started:

DO . . . help each child become aware of his or her heritage.

DO . . . ask for help from family members and people in the community.

DO . . . consider starting with the cultures represented by children in your classroom.

DO . . . use sources (people and material) that represent the perspective of the group under study.

DON'T . . . expect to have right away all the books, videos, and artifacts that you need to really bring a unit of study alive. Assume that each year you will acquire one or two outstanding new materials.

DON'T . . . neglect to do some research of your own on the group of people your children will be studying.

DON'T . . . be afraid to start with your own culture and heritage!

DON'T . . . forget to read aloud daily to children from literature that fairly represents the culture you are studying.

Goals

Multicultural programs are as diverse as the cultures they represent. However, some general goals pertain to all.

- **Avoid stereotyping.** One way to do this is to be sure you represent every culture *as it is in the present,* as well as how it was in the past. All cultures are in a continual state of change.

- **Put the literature to work for you.** A large part of your daily activities can be reading or listening to a story, song, or poem and then responding to it.

- **Accentuate your children's languages, backgrounds, and cultures.** Exploring even the trappings of a culture—festivals, dances, costumes, artifacts, foods—can help young children better understand and appreciate the attitudes and beliefs that define a particular culture.

- **Highlight the contributions *all* groups have made.** Find and share information about scientific, artistic, and social achievements by diverse members of society.

- **Remember that multicultural ideas are "caught" rather than "taught."** The attitudes you are trying to develop in children cannot be taught in formal lessons. They come through everyday experiences in which respect for others is the goal.

- **Promote fair-mindedness.** Encourage children to think critically with open minds that respect differing viewpoints.

"**M**ulticultural education involves changes in the total school or educational environment; it is not limited to curricular changes."

James Banks
Multicultural Education: Issues and Perspectives

Integrating READING STRATEGIES

by Dr. Dorothy S. Strickland

Reading strategically is about making sense of what you read. As teachers, we need to provide daily activities that require children to integrate reading strategies and skills until they are internalized, natural behaviors. Reading and writing are strategic when children know both the strategy and the time and place to use it.

Shared Reading

Many strategies and skills are modeled as teacher and children work together to read a text. Children have an opportunity to try out what they know in a risk-free environment. Some examples of common opportunities for teachers to highlight reading strategies during shared reading are making predictions, noting details, identifying cause and effect, and summarizing.

Response Journals

Children may offer a free response or respond to a prompt given by the teacher, such as this: *Think about the two main characters, Jack and Ted. Tell how they are alike and how they are different.* In order to respond, children must recall details, compare and contrast, and make inferences. All are key comprehension strategies.

Book Discussion Groups

Discussion after reading frequently centers on the responses children have made in their response journals. When children read their responses aloud, teachers have an opportunity to learn how they have internalized information and expressed their own ideas. During discussion, children have an opportunity to draw on all their strategies for reading. Some examples are making judgments, identifying main ideas, classifying information, and drawing conclusions.

Literature Mapping

Even at the simplest levels, mapping stories allows children to reorganize information and classify it into key components. Here is an example to try: Give each child a large piece of construction paper divided into thirds. Have the children label each section *beginning, middle,* or *ending,* or label the paper for them. Then have them draw a picture about the part of the story that fits in each box and write a sentence or two about it at the bottom of the box.

This activity requires children to recall information, sequence events, and retell events in their own words.

Harcourt Brace School Publishers

ASSESSING A CHILD'S ORAL READING

Listening to children read aloud offers opportunities to observe their use of some reading strategies:

- **Is the reading fluent?** Smooth reading indicates good comprehension.
- **Is appropriate expression used?** Inappropriate expression or a lack of expression during oral reading may mean the child does not understand what is being pronounced.
- **Does the child self-correct to preserve meaning?** This indicates that the child is self-monitoring his or her reading.
- **Does the child take risks in pronunciation?** A child who feels confident about using phonics and context clues together will usually give an unknown word a reasonable try. Children's attempts tell a great deal about the way they are processing text.
- **Does the child use strategies appropriately?** Through modeling and discussion, children should be helped to apply some of the following strategies when confronting unknown words:

  Skip the word and continue to read. Perhaps more information will give you a clue.

  Reread the sentence to see what might make sense.

  Use the information in the story and context clues in the sentence to help figure out what the word might be.

  Use picture clues.

  Try sounding out the word, keeping in mind what might make sense.

> **"Effective reading instruction emphasizes the teaching of strategies (and their attendant skills) as integrated processes rather than a set of discrete subskills."**

Often-Asked Questions About Vocabulary Development

by Dr. W. Dorsey Hammond

Dr. W. Dorsey Hammond, Professor of Education at Oakland University in Rochester, Michigan, is a recognized authority on comprehension and vocabulary development in children.

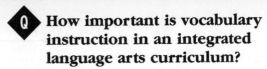 **How important is vocabulary instruction in an integrated language arts curriculum?**

A Vocabulary instruction is very important. However, we need to look at vocabulary in a broader context. We should think of vocabulary in terms of language development. People with good vocabularies don't just know the meanings of many words; they have versatility with language. They use the right word for the right occasion. They have *variety* and *flexibility* in language and word usage. That's why vocabulary is best developed in the context of literature and all of the language arts.

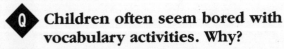 **Children often seem bored with vocabulary activities. Why?**

A Sometimes children are bored because they see no reason for the vocabulary activities they are doing. The activities are separate from the stories they are reading and writing. Or sometimes, children are required to look up lists of words in dictionaries and write each word in a sentence. Other children are asked to memorize definitions. These activities simply don't work, and children tend to understand that.

Q **How can we improve our children's vocabulary and language?**

A We begin with a basic truth. Children and adults who read a great deal tend to have good vocabularies. The best way to improve vocabulary is to have a strong reading and writing curriculum. It's true, of course, that we need vocabulary in order to read; it's also very true that as we read, we increase our vocabulary and versatility with language.

Q **Can vocabulary be developed through direct instruction?**

A Yes, as long as it's taught in a meaningful context.

Can you give an example of teaching vocabulary in a meaningful context?

 After children finish reading a story, ask them to pick out two or three words or phrases that they found the most interesting, and discuss them.

 Are you saying that the best time to develop vocabulary is after the reading?

 In most cases, yes. Then it is meaningful and in context. As children respond to a story, they can talk about interesting language, new words, old words with new meanings, and so on.

 Don't children need to know the meanings of all the words in order to understand a story?

 They need to know the meanings of most words, but not all. In order to decide which words to teach children before reading a text or story, use the following key:

1. Word is essential for story comprehension and is not defined in context.
2. Word is essential but is defined in context.
3. Word is not necessary for adequate comprehension.
4. Word is not necessary but is an interesting word or phrase.

If condition 1 prevails, teach the word or phrase *before* reading and review it after reading. If condition 2, 3, or 4 prevails, it's probably better to address these words and phrases after reading.

 Can you give examples of words defined in context?

 Sure. Look at the following sentences: "Imagine a line of a thousand camels, one after the other, carrying salt, silk, and tea across the desert. Such caravans . . . ." Notice how we are given the definition and then provided the label. Or in this example: "The castle is surrounded by a water-filled ditch called a moat." In this example, we have an explicit definition of a moat.

The important issue here is that we raise this context strategy with our children. We need to teach children not only *about* language but also *how* language works in authentic texts.

 What are some basic guidelines for developing vocabulary?

 1. Teach in context whenever possible.
2. Talk about words: interesting words, unusual words, new words, old words with new meanings.
3. Teach children how to use context to figure out unfamiliar words.
4. Focus on just a few words. It's better to learn three words well than ten words superficially.
5. Promote words. Have a wall chart with the three or four most interesting words children have read or heard this week.
6. Think in terms of phrases and sentences and interesting sayings.
7. Use literature as a model of how words might be used. Good authors are masters at choosing just the right word.
8. Promote variety and versatility. Talk about how even a simple word can have many meanings. An example is the word *track:* a track for jogging, a railroad track, to track a deer, on the right track, and so on.
9. Compliment children when they use interesting language in their conversation and writing.
10. Remember, words aren't just learned or unlearned. Sometimes we understand a word in depth. For some words we have an average understanding. For other words we "sort of" know what the word means but can't really explain it.

Harcourt Brace School Publishers

Achieving BALANCE in Our Literacy Programs

by Dr. Dorothy S. Strickland

The State of New Jersey Professor of Reading, Rutgers University

New insights into learning and teaching have brought about numerous changes in literacy instruction in recent years, particularly in the early grades.

Greater emphasis on writing and its relationship to reading, greater use of trade books, and increased attention to the integration of the language arts are among the most noticeable changes. Most would agree that there is much to celebrate. But, as with anything new, the changes have also brought about some confusion and frustration. A variety of factors may account for this.

- **At times, new ideas were embraced and implemented before they were clearly understood.**

- **At other times, change was only nominally accepted and more-familiar methods were imposed on the new curricular frameworks and materials.**

- **In still other cases, too many changes were imposed at once.**

As a result, many educators were made to feel as though they were struggling in a morass of change.

Today, in districts throughout the country, educators are once again reexamining the direction they have taken. They are wondering, "Have we gone too far in one direction or another? Have we abandoned some of the tried and true good practices of the past?" They want to know how they can take advantage of the best research and practice available today in a way that makes sense and is more effective for children, teachers, and parents. They are searching for balance.

When educators search for balance in their literacy programs, certain issues inevitably surface. Following is a list of some of these issues and suggestions for how they might be addressed.

BALANCING A *SKILLS* EMPHASIS WITH A *MEANING* EMPHASIS

Neither skills nor meaning need ever be abandoned. Indeed, skills are learned best when taught through meaningful use. For example, after sharing a story that includes many examples of the same sound/letter relationship, such as /b/*b* or the inflectional ending *-ing,* point out the relationship and discuss it with children. Help them make a chart of other examples they find in their reading, and encourage them to use what they have learned in their own writing.

Harcourt Brace School Publishers

BALANCING DIRECT AND INDIRECT INSTRUCTION

Direct instruction usually refers to the explicit transmission of knowledge. Indirect instruction involves providing opportunities for children to discover new ideas and strategies, to apply skills they have learned, and to assist one another as teachers and learners. Effective teaching will make use of both. For example, minilessons are key elements of contemporary literacy instruction. These are systematically planned, brief instructional episodes that focus on a single strategy for learning and that employ direct instructional methods. Minilessons make heavy use of the modeling and demonstration of skills. Teachers not only *tell;* they *show.* Showing how something is done is one of the most effective methods of direct instruction available. Still, that is not enough. For children to "own" a skill or strategy, they need opportunities to try it out on their own and to "discover" opportunities for its use. The most adept teachers are those who know how to provide a variety of opportunities for children to learn and to apply their learning in a meaningful way.

BALANCING CONTENT AND PROCESS

Although the desire for information frequently inspires us to learn, learning involves much more than accumulating information. If we overemphasize content, children are left not knowing how to get information or to learn on their own. When teachers plan for instruction in science or social studies, for example, they need to keep both content and process goals in mind.

Content goals refer to the knowledge we hope children will gain from the topic under study, such as how plants grow or the kinds of helpers in the neighborhood. **Process goals** refer to what we hope children will be able to do at the end of the study—specifically, how to observe and chart the growth of a seedling over a period of time or how to interview a neighborhood helper and write a brief paragraph to share with the class.

Process goals take children beyond the specific subject matter, helping them become skillful learners no matter what content is under study.

BALANCING TRADE BOOKS AND TEXTBOOKS

In many school districts, textbooks continue to be the core materials in various curricular areas, providing a sense of continuity across grade levels. An effective literacy program embraces a wide variety of materials, including separately bound trade books. It may be helpful to think in terms of several layers of texts in the classroom. One layer might involve the literature selected by the teacher for read-aloud purposes. Another might be the core literacy program in which all children

Harcourt Brace School Publishers

are involved, providing many opportunities for extension to trade books and technology. Yet another layer might involve a variety of self-selected materials that children read independently. While these layers relate specifically to the literacy program, children should be involved with both core and trade book materials in every subject area. Each layer has an important role to play in a balanced program of instruction.

BALANCING INFORMAL CLASSROOM ASSESSMENT AND NORM-REFERENCED STANDARDIZED TESTS

Shifting the balance away from standardized tests in favor of authentic classroom assessment methods is a goal that most educators applaud. Standardized tests are useful in rank-ordering pupils and, frequently, teachers and schools as well. However, they do little to help teachers focus on instructional needs. Schools are seeking to make greater use of performance-based assessment procedures, which are closely linked to the curriculum and also serve to inform the public about

how well students are doing. For example, portfolios that include samples of a child's writing over time help both teacher and child get a sense of specific strengths and weaknesses. Probably most important, this type of ongoing assessment tends to make the criteria more clear to both child and teacher.

Achieving balance in our literacy programs should not imply that there is such a thing as "The Balanced Approach." Nor should it imply a sampling method in which a teacher selects a little of this and a little of that. Finally, it should not imply two very distinct, parallel approaches coexisting in a single classroom—for example, literature on Mondays and Wednesdays and skills the remainder of the week.

Ultimately, a teacher must make instructional decisions based on how children learn and how he or she can best teach them. More than likely this will never mean throwing out all of the methods used by any single teacher or school district. Needless to say, it will also not mean maintaining the status quo. Finding the balance takes knowledge, time, and thoughtfulness. ●

Harcourt Brace School Publishers

Tips for No-Fuss Story Dramatization

By

Dr. W. Dorsey Hammond

"Creative drama activities provide valid reasons to read, write, speak, and listen and become the vehicle for integrating these other areas."

Karen Kutiper
Ideas for Creative Teaching

As teachers, we look for ways to make stories come alive for children. Drama is a particularly effective way to make a story concrete and real because the children themselves are actively involved in re-creating the story. Yet some educators shy away from dramatizing stories or even parts of stories, thinking they have to do costumes, props, and scenery. Nothing could be further from the truth! Wonderful drama experiences can happen with little or no preparation and no extra materials. All you need is a good story and your children's creative input.

Start Simple!

Participation Stories   During a participation story, children gesture or make sounds at appropriate moments during the narration. While listening to "The Three Billy-Goats Gruff," for example, children might help make the *trip-trap* sound of the bridge. Or, during a reading of *Where the Wild Things Are*, children might be asked to "show their terrible claws" whenever they hear that phrase.

Great Stories for Participation
Caps for Sale by Esphyr Slobodkina. Addison-Wesley, 1947.
Cock-A-Doodle Do! by Harriet Ziefert. HarperCollins, 1986.
The Enormous Turnip by Kathy Parkinson. Whitman, 1985.
The Cow That Went Oink by Bernard Most. Harcourt Brace, 1990.
Good-Night, Owl! by Pat Hutchins. Macmillan, 1972.
Run! Run! by Harriet Ziefert. HarperCollins, 1986.
Where the Wild Things Are by Maurice Sendak. HarperCollins, 1963.

Choral Speaking   Good material for choral speaking includes songs, poetry, rhymes, and stories with repetitive lines. Let children help decide the parts, inflections, volume, and expression for each selection. Use a big book version of a story, or make a chart so that everyone can easily follow along.

Great Stories for Choral Speaking
Brown Bear, Brown Bear, What Do You See? by Bill Martin, Jr. Henry Holt, 1992.
Chicka Chicka Boom Boom by Bill Martin, Jr. and John Archambault. Simon & Schuster, 1989.
Drummer Hoff adapted by Barbara Emberley. Prentice Hall, 1967.
Five Little Monkeys Sitting in a Tree by Eileen Christelow. Clarion, 1991.
Four Fur Feet by Margaret Wise Brown. Addison-Wesley, 1989.
One Cow Moo Moo! by David Bennett. Henry Holt, 1990.
Over in the Meadow by Ezra Jack Keats. Scholastic, 1992.
Silly Sally by Audrey Wood. Harcourt Brace, 1992.

Acting Out Stories   What child doesn't enjoy pretending to be a big bad wolf or a quick-witted gingerbread man? A group of children can re-enact "The Three Little Pigs" in less than five minutes. The only advance preparation needed is a group brainstorming session to map out areas of the room for the story's beginning (Mother Pig's house), middle (building the houses, meeting the wolf), and ending ("And the wolf ran away, never to be seen again. THE END.").

Harcourt Brace School Publishers

The key to successful playacting with young children is to familiarize them thoroughly with the story first. Several choral readings of a story are useful here because children will chime in on repeated phrases during the rereadings. In effect, they're already rehearsing their lines!

When choosing a story for children to dramatize, look for

- few characters and characters with obvious personality traits.
- a clear story line.
- exciting dramatic conflict.
- repetitive phrases or situations.

You will be amazed (and amused) by children's ability to improvise lines, role-play characters' actions, and recall details. The first few dramatizations will probably require you to narrate the action fairly closely. Pause often to allow children to fill in characters' dialogue and to act out events. As the class becomes more proficient at playacting, encourage them to take over more and more of the production.

Great Stories for Acting Out

Anansi the Spider: A Tale from the Ashanti by Gerald McDermott. Henry Holt, 1972.

Eeney, Meeney, Miney, Mo by B. G. Hennessy. Viking, 1993.

Hello, House! by Linda Hayward. Random House, 1988.

The Little Red Hen by Patricia McKissack. Childrens Press, 1985.

Skyfire by Frank Asch. Prentice Hall, 1988.

Instant Drama Activities

Creating Images As you read or tell children a story, pause on occasion and ask them to describe the pictures they see in their heads. Encourage children to use their imaginations. Here's an example:

As the prince rode toward the castle on his horse . . .

| Teacher: | What do you see? |
| Student 1: | He's riding this horse. |

Teacher:	What does it look like to you?
Student 2:	It's a black horse. It's galloping.
Student 3:	And it has lots of shiny stuff on the saddle.
Student 4:	Shiny metal like silver.
Teacher:	Tell us about the castle. What do you see?
Student 2:	It has flags flying on top.
Student 4:	It's made of big stones, and it's on this hill.
Student 5:	I see a big wooden gate in front with chains. And there are two guards outside. . . .

Remember, the ability to create images in one's head is an important factor in comprehension. Students need to *visualize* what is happening as they read. Ask students to describe how a particular character looks or how he or she is dressed. Encourage young children to draw pictures of story events, scenes, and characters, thus integrating art, drama, and reading.

In addition, encourage students to illustrate stories they read and stories they write. This will promote the imaging process.

Role-Playing and Improvisation

Sometimes we may want children to dramatize a scene or even just a phrase. For example,

Marsha crept into the bedroom so no one would hear her.

Teacher: Who would like to show us how Marsha did that?

Sam's eyes followed the man as he crossed the street.

Teacher: Let's see how Sam did that. Who would like to show us?

Harcourt Brace School Publishers

Phrases or Scenes to Dramatize
Be out of breath.
Watch a plane fly overhead.
Train a lion.
Paint a wall.
Peel a banana.
Type on a computer.

Interpretive Reading Encourage children to reread selected passages for interpretation. Conversation between characters is a natural area for interpretation. For example, the conversation in *The Day Jimmy's Boa Ate the Wash* lends itself to interpretive reading:

> "How was your class trip to the farm?"
> "Oh . . . boring . . . kind of dull . . . until the cow started crying."
> "A cow . . . crying?"
> "Yeah, you see, a haystack fell on her . . . ."

Imagine the enjoyment children would have rereading this conversation between a mother and her unflappable child!

Round-Robin Storytelling After children have read or heard a story a few times, have them sit in a circle. Hold a prop from the story in your hand, and begin to retell the story. Pause after a few sentences and pass the prop to a child next to you, who then continues the tale. The prop is passed around the circle as children continue the tale to the end.

Great Stories and Easy Props for Round-Robin Storytelling
Arthur's Valentine by Marc Brown. Little, Brown, 1980. (Use a fancy paper heart.)
Corduroy by Don Freeman. Viking, 1968. (Use a teddy bear.)
Imogene's Antlers by David Small. Crown, 1986. (Use paper or cloth antlers.)
Olive and the Magic Hat by Eileen Christelow. Clarion, 1987. (Use a top hat.)
Princess Smartypants by Babette Cole. G. P. Putnam's Sons, 1987. (Use a crown.)
The Snowy Day by Ezra Jack Keats. Viking, 1962. (Use a pair of mittens.)

Drama demands the best from children—they have to solve problems on their feet, learn to work together, analyze characters' motivations and feelings, and take apart a piece of literature and then put it back together with their bodies and their words. Best of all, it's a lot of fun for children *and* for their teacher. ∎

Harcourt Brace School Publishers

PHONICS:
It's not just for reading time anymore

by Dr. Nancy Roser
Professor, Language and Literacy Studies, University of Texas at Austin

If the ceaseless debate about young children's literacy learning could be softened for just a moment to more conversational tones, if the mythology and rhetoric could be momentarily ignored, if the evidence could be reviewed from the perspectives of all kinds of learners, the conversants might just admit they agree upon some things. Among those agreements would be this:

For children to grow into independent, fluent readers, they will need to understand that their written language is not a random system. Rather, the sounds of their language—its words and messages—are represented by letters in ways that, if not totally consistent, work in somewhat predictable and patterned ways.

Even so, the passion that fuels the debate about beginners' literacy will last—as long as the rhetoric focuses on how and when kids achieve this agreed-upon understanding. Well-intentioned grown-ups are certain they know "truths" for all young learners about how literacy should be taught. The truth is, however, that the realities of classrooms should humble us all.

May I introduce you to two children from those real classrooms? You may feel that you already know them. One is six; the other seven. One is a girl; the other a boy. One is poor; the other isn't. Both are adept with friends. Both love stories. Both smile easily and often. Both have loving families and give spontaneous hugs. Even though they share a geographic community, their cultural heritages are different, and their understanding of how print works seems to differ by light-years.

In the drawing, the child's thought bubble reads:

My thos udat
Penuts.

A Penut is Lic a Luch-
Box Becus tha bth ca-
ree food.

Penut

Apple   Samwich

"Some thoughts about peanuts," Holly says to her paper. And her hand moves across the page so rapidly that even a novice observer can tell that she is comfortable with her self-selected task. She has internalized the sound-symbol correspondences that allow her to record her language in ways that communicate with others.

First, meet Holly. A first grader, Holly is dauntless in her approach to literacy learning. She is a reader of simple books by the second month of first grade. At home and at school, she is keenly interested in stories—especially those with incongruities that tickle her funny bone. She had memorized some of her favorite books by the time she was three, probably because of the number of times she requested, "Read it again." Just last week, her mom finished reading *Charlotte's Web* to her. Emerging as a conventional reader, Holly also believes and acts confidently upon her hypothesis that what she can say, she can write. And she writes often—all across her day for all kinds of reasons, including simply to show what she's thinking.

She talks as she writes, but prosodically, rather than with the hesitant, effortful pace of a child who is still building notions of how code works and practicing matchups of phoneme with grapheme. Holly does not use the beginning writer's useful strategy of slowing speech to distinguish separate sounds. Instead, Holly is chatting: "A peanut is like a lunch box. They both carry food." Her voice lifts in decided exclamation at the end. Then she illustrates her analogy. As rapidly as she writes, she draws a peanut shell holding three seeds and then a transparent lunch box containing both apple and "samwich." Smiling triumphantly, she claims her work: "by Holly 6yersood." Through the right confluence of variables, Holly is achieving literacy.

Now meet another child you may feel you know. Chris, a second grader, is also joyous about schooling, eager to work, comfortable with copying, curious about stories, and especially intrigued by messages being written by his teacher. Even so, after two years of books and writing and instruction with letters and sounds, as Chris faces print, he's unsure of words he's seen repeatedly. Words such as *yes, no, me,* and *jump* leave him puzzled. He grins shyly and says, "I used to know those words, Miss. My mom, she told them to me." And he did. And she had. Almost all his book experiences have been school experiences, but his

Harcourt Brace School Publishers

home life is enriched by family stories that he shares. Chris hasn't yet associated authors with books, but that doesn't seem to diminish his pleasure in story time. Just last week, after rereading a Big Book with his classmates and talking over the print they noticed, Chris set to work building sentences that included some of the story words. Sitting next to him, his teacher directed his attention to the first letter in *no*. He got to use his knowledge about that letter to try to read the word. He compared *no* with *on* and got to explain how two tiny words with the same letters could end up so differently. Friends leaned over his desk to point things out. He kept smiling. But the next day, the letter *n*'s name was gone. So was the sound he needed in order to unlock *no*.

Chris can't yet tell what sound comes at the beginning of fish or at the end of words like hat and cat. Rhyming isn't easy for him, either, but he's catching on. "I used to know that, Miss," he says.

When these children are your students, you know just what to do for Holly—surround her with book and print opportunities and with reasons to read and write. Make conversation about written messages of all sorts. Investigate intriguing topics so that she can learn *through* her developing literacy skills. Show her more and more ways she can use the regularity of her written language system, as well as its quirkiness. Read to her; read with her; write to her; write with her. Encourage her to read and write with others. Let her elaborate and publish her writing, attending to more and more of the conventions of print. Create opportunities for her to retell, respond, enact, and share her literacy. All day long, point out how her language works.

But what do you do for Chris? He does not yet recognize the words in his stories or match sounds with letters. His writing is still made up of strings of letters. He does not operate with awareness that his spoken language is made up of separate sounds. (See also "Phonemic Awareness," on page 18.) Chris needs *all* the book and print and purposeful writing opportunities that Holly does; the goals are the same. He needs simple, memorable texts read aloud to him and chances to reread those books. He needs chances to innovate on verses, to sing and match his voice with the words on a chart. Chris needs chances to point to and talk about print, to build words with magnetic letters, to experiment with their patterns, and to write with groups of friends who can help him encode his messages. He, too, needs a classroom teacher who throughout the day's instructional activities points out how language works. In addition, Chris needs to operate playfully with the sounds of his language—to chime in on rhythmic texts, to substitute sounds for nonsensical fun, to learn that he can take words apart and put them back together again. As my friend Debbie Price says, "Chris needs explicit demonstrations, invitations, and explanations all day long."

Ways to give explicit help all day long

LANGUAGE PLAY Because children love language, rhythm, and rhyme, it makes sense that their classroom days are filled with chants, songs, and verses. Happily, participating with and manipulating the sounds of language propels literacy as well. Bobbi Fisher (1991) offers her children from four to six familiar songs, poems, or chants each day. As the children sing along, tap along, and chant along, they are building understandings of the way language works (and plays).

Let children innovate on their texts, as below: [From Sue Williams's *I Went Walking* (Harcourt Brace, 1991)]

Text: I went walking.
What did you see?
I saw a black cat
Looking at me.

Children: I went walking and
what did I see?
A great big green frog
Jumping at me!

Let them innovate with sounds, too:

Teacher: If the giant hadn't said,
"Fee-fie-foe-fum!"
he might have said . . .

Child: "Cree-cry-cro-crum!"

Child: "Bee-by-bo-bum!"

Child: "Me-my-mo-mum?"

PRINT TALK Just as there must be sound play, so must there be talk about print. Talk about all kinds of print in all kinds of places—on signs, on charts, in Big Books, in read-alouds, on notes and letters, in science records, on math graphs, on community bulletin boards, in library books, in textbooks, and in journals. Use ubiquitous print for continuing talk: "What do you notice?" "What do

you see?" "How does it work there?" "How do you know?"

Children learn how print works when you model by writing to them and for them—morning messages, surprises, announcements, reminders. Here's how the talk goes in a class in which Teacher is writing the name of the book she is just about to read aloud [*Suddenly!* by Colin McNaughton (Harcourt Brace, 1994)]:

Harcourt Brace School Publishers

Teacher writes:	The voices of children respond:
S	S! /s! S! /s/ Swimmy!
SUD	S-U-D /s/ Sam!
	Sam the Rose Horse!
	Starts like: /s/ /uhd/ Sud . . .
SUDDEN	D! Dog! No! /d/ /d/ /en/ Sud . . . /d/ den. Sudden!
SUDDENLY!	/l/ . . . /i/ /ly/! Suddenly!

SPECIAL EQUIPMENT Teachers have all sorts of favorite materials for working with sounds and their symbols. First graders in Patti Bridwell's class rely on Sound Signs posted around the room. When they are sounding *Down the Road,* their eyes can search for the *ou, ow* sign—the one with the bandage on it (OW!). Many teachers rely on cardboard or heavy-stock frames or windows that allow their children and them to focus on the print they notice and want to talk about. Bobbi Fisher suggests the frames be of differing sizes to accommodate talk about letters as well as long words. Other favorite materials are letter card sets, individual chalkboards, object boxes, and magnet letters on cookie sheets.

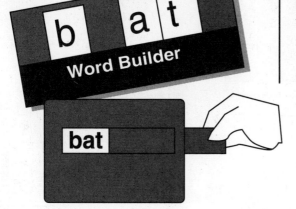

SPECIAL ACTIVITIES Try using a simple variation of the Cunningham's Make-a-Word Technique by letting children build words (short ones and long ones) with a preselected set of letter cards while you direct and monitor. It can work like this:

- "Use two letters to make *at.*" (Children align *a* and *t.* A successful child demonstrates with the Word Builder; less-successful children get help from peers.)
- "Now use three letters to make *bat.*"

Depending on skill and ability, children can steadily increase the length of the words they build, rearrange the letters to form still other words, and even learn to return to the pile of letters that are no longer needed. Gunning (1995) suggests building words with the highest-frequency phonogram patterns. Building words provides a good opportunity for talking about useful spelling patterns, such as "magic *e*" or consonants that often travel together.

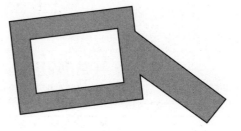

HIGH-FREQUENCY PHONOGRAMS

-ad	-ank	-ed	-ide	-ock	-ow
-ag	-ap	-eed	-ig	-og	-oy
-ail	-ar	-eel	-ight	-oke	-ub
-ain	-are	-eep	-ike	-old	-ug
-air	-ark	-eer	-ill	-ook	-um
-ake	-at	-en	-im	-op	-ump
-all	-ate	-ent	-in	-ope	-un
-ame	-aw	-est	-ind	-ore	-up
-an	-ay	-et	-ing	-orn	-urry
-and	-ead	-ew	-ip	-ot	-ust
-ang	-ear	-id	-it	-ound	-ut

Harcourt Brace School Publishers

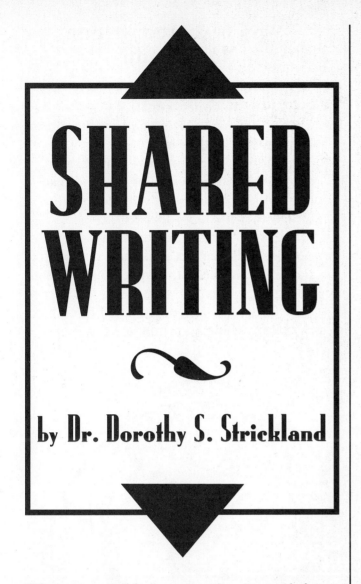

SHARED WRITING

by Dr. Dorothy S. Strickland

"If we want Ashley's mom to come and show us how to plant our garden, how can we let her know?" Janiece Turner looked out at her second graders as hands flew in the air to respond.

"Ask Ashley to tell her," replied Josh.

"Call her up," answered Angel.

"Is there anything else we might do?" asked Janiece.

"Well, I guess we could write her a letter," Tonya responded.

"We certainly could," said Janiece. "And we can do it together."

Janiece went to the easel, flipped to a clean sheet of chart paper, and began an interactive process in which she and the children went back and forth, making decisions about what to say, how it might be spelled, and where it should go.

"How do we start?"

Someone suggested *Dear Mrs. Benton.* "Does anyone besides Ashley know how *Benton* begins?"

"Yes, with a *B,*" someone offered.

"Good, James. Will you spell the rest of your name for us, Ashley? Notice that I'm putting a comma after *Benton.* Now, it would be very nice to include the date on our letter. Does anyone have any idea where we should put it? Who can help us spell *March?*"

The process continues until a draft of the letter is completed. The children review what they have said. Janiece asks for comments about changes. Later, she will enter the letter in the computer and have one or two children decorate the stationery before it goes home with Ashley. Janiece will hang the draft in the library corner for the children to read at their leisure.

> "Shared writing provides a risk-free opportunity for children to engage in the writing process."

What is shared writing?

Shared writing is an interactive group writing process in which teachers and children work together to compose or record meaningful messages and stories. The teacher often acts as a scribe as he or she thinks through with children what they want to say and the best way to say it. Individual children may also act as scribes as they fill in letters and words that they know. Everyone works together to draft, revise, and edit as appropriate. Shared writing provides a risk-free opportunity for children to engage in the writing process.

Any kind of writing may be the focus of shared writing: response to reading, group stories, big books, poems, informational notes and books, class charts, and written retellings are just a few.

Why is shared writing important?

- Writing is shown to be a functional, meaningful way to communicate.
- Teachers model reading and writing during the creation of the text.
- The entire writing process, from brainstorming during prewriting to proofreading and editing, may be modeled to the extent that it is appropriate.
- A variety of writing strategies are developed as children get first-hand demonstrations and rehearsal from participating with others.
- Specific skills may be explained in context as children help to produce a finished piece.

Harcourt Brace School Publishers

What happens during shared writing?

Prewriting

Stimulus   Shared writing is generally stimulated by a common experience of some kind, such as a class trip, a school assembly, or a book that the teacher has read aloud to the whole group.

Discussion   Actual writing is usually preceded by a brief discussion: Who is our audience? What form of writing should we use? What should we say?

Drafting

Writing   The teacher guides children as they "think through" the process together. The teacher acts as a scribe, demonstrates the conventions of writing, and uses prompts to help children explore possible ideas for their text.

Revision/Proofreading

Refining   Throughout the writing, the teacher constantly solicits help by asking questions and thinking aloud about needed wording, punctuation, spelling, and so on. Upon completion of the piece, the teacher and children review it together for final polishing.

OPPORTUNITIES FOR SHARED WRITING

- Group retellings
    Story read aloud
    Facts remembered from a
      nonfiction text
- Group compositions
    Original stories
    Big books
    Alternative texts based on stories
      read aloud
    Poetry
- Class charts
    Class jobs
    Class rules
    Directions
- Captions for displays
    Books by Cynthia Rylant
    Shells found on the beach
    Our baby pictures

Stages in Emergent Writing

by Patricia Smith

Not long ago, many educators believed children had to be well versed in reading and "readiness" skills before they could write. We now know these facts:

- Children know much more about print at an earlier age than we gave them credit for in the past.

- Children discover that writing is oral language in written form. What can be said can also be written.

- Emergent writers experiment with writing long before they're independent readers, and what they learn about print from shared reading is reflected in what and how they write. Reading and writing develop together.

- Young children who see writing modeled at home and at school are eager to try it on their own and quickly come to view themselves as writers with something important to say.

Harcourt Brace School Publishers

Beginning writers progress through predictable, recognizable stages that will vary in duration for individual children. Since these stages are not rigid, examples from more than one of the following stages will often appear in the same piece of writing:

1. **Scribbling,** or pretend writing, is not necessarily random marks on the page (Figure 1). It may be a child's first attempt to approximate the print he or she encounters naturally all day long. Listen for the running monologue that may accompany a child's scribbling; this child is well aware that written symbols contain meaning!

2. **Letter strings,** or random letters, are a child's attempts to mimic the forms of our alphabet (Figure 2). At this prephonemic stage, letters do not yet represent sounds. More often than not, the child uses capital letters. You may notice that a child at this stage is already practicing left-to-right and top-to-bottom progression on the page.

3. **One-letter spelling** is a common occurrence in the early phonemic stage (Figure 3). Here a child uses the initial consonant, and perhaps another distinctive consonant, to represent an entire word, such as *b* for *baby* or *bl* for *believe.*

4. **Invented spelling** is a window on a child's understanding of sound-symbol correspondences (Figure 4). Children who are encouraged to "spell a word the best they can" experiment with beginning and ending consonants and often with medial sounds as well. Usually, vowels come much later although all-important words like *I* and *a* appear early in a child's writing vocabulary.

5. **Transitional spelling** is the stage in which children adjust their own simple spelling rules (*shz* for *shoes, wans* for *once*) to accommodate what they're learning from their reading (Figure 5).

Features such as double consonants and silent letters also begin to appear.

6. **Conventional spelling** begins to appear in a few high-frequency words written by young primary children. As these children continue through the primary grades, more words are written with conventional spelling.

Promoting Conventional Spelling

Consider developing a poster with the following information to support conventional spelling.

SPELLING STEPS

1. Say the word softly.
2. Think of the sounds you hear.
3. Write the word.
4. Look at your word.
5. Make changes if it does not look right.
6. Look at it again. If it appears right, go on. If not . . .
7. Use help from
    - a place where the word is already printed.
    - a person who can help you spell the word.
8. Write the word correctly on your paper and in your spelling journal.

Keep in Mind . . .

Remember that we want our children to use the best words they can think of, even if they are unable to spell the words correctly. Reassure children that you will be able to read or hear them read what they have written. Tell children that having their thoughts in written form is what you want *most of all.*

When it appears that children are moving into transitional and conventional spelling, you can support their spelling efforts by

- allowing children to help one another achieve more conventional spelling.

Harcourt Brace School Publishers

- teaching letter-sound associations.
- teaching the correct spelling of high-frequency words.
- creating a print-rich environment that includes banks of words that might be used in writing.
- supplying children with personal spelling journals in which they can write new words on alphabetized pages.
- showing children how to circle in early drafts the words with which they want spelling assistance.
- reassuring children that while you are proud of their growing spelling abilities, you understand that they may not be able to spell the words used by older writers.

Management Tip

Trim chart paper the width of a coat hanger. Let children attach their own word banks to hangers. Hang the word banks in the coat closet for easy storage and retrieval when needed. The charts can be hung near children who need the spelling help.

Some children have extensive experience with writing before they enter school; others may be experimenting with crayons and pencils for the first time. You can promote children's emergent writing by

- modeling writing behaviors every day.
- providing writing supplies in learning centers.
- encouraging children to make their own signs, lists, recording sheets, captions, and so on when they need them.
- setting aside time for children to keep personal journals, to write individual and group stories, and to respond to literature in writing.
- celebrating the efforts of emergent writers.

Figure 1

Figure 2

Figure 3

Figure 4

Figure 5

Harcourt Brace School Publishers

The Synchrony of Reading and Spelling Development:
HOW CHILDREN LEARN ABOUT WORDS

by Dr. Donald R. Bear Dr. Bear is Professor and Director of the Center for Learning and Literacy at the College of Education, University of Nevada, Reno.

OLD MISTER RABBIT
D. Lipman

1. Old Mister Rabbit,
You've got a mighty
habit,
Of jumping in my
garden
And eating all my
cabbage.

2. Old Mister Rabbit,
You've got a mighty
habit,
Of jumping in my
garden
And eating all my
broccoli.

3. Old Mister Rabbit,
You've got a mighty
habit,
Of jumping in my
garden
And eating all my
tomatoes.

4. Old Mister Rabbit,
You've got a mighty
habit,
Of jumping in my
garden
And eating all my ice
cream.

If you were to choral read "Old Mister Rabbit" a few times with your children and then ask individuals to try to read it independently, could you predict which of them would be able to? Children in the emergent stage of literacy could do a fair job *approximating* the text, based on their familiarity with it.

Children who cannot reliably track text by pointing with a finger as they read would have particular difficulty tracking two-syllable words. For example, in the phrase *Old Mister Rabbit,* they might say /tur/ when pointing to *Rabbit,* thinking it was the second syllable in *Mister.* A child's ability to track print tells a lot about his or her concept of word (Morris, 1981). Not surprisingly, it also helps us identify his or her stage of spelling development.

Figure 1. Synchrony of Literacy Development

Reading Stages and Behaviors

Emergent	*Beginning*		*Transitional*

No concept of word
Pretend reading
	Rudimentary concept
	  of word
	Reads with support
	Disfluent and
	  unexpressive reading
	Finger-point reading
	Reads aloud to self
		Functional concept
		  of word
		Reads longer passages
		  with support
			Approaching fluency
			Reads easy chapter
			  books

Stages of Spelling and Word Study Activities

Preliterate Stage	*Early Letter-Name Stage*	*Letter-Name Stage*	*Within-Word-Pattern Stage*

Examples
  Scribbles
	B or *BD* for *bed*
	D, J, G, JR, or *DRV*
	  for *drive*
	F, FL, or *FLT* for *float*
		BAD for *bed*
		JRIV, DIV, or *DRIV* for
		  drive
		FOT or *FLOT* for *float*
			Spells *bed* correctly
			DRIEV or spells *drive*
			  correctly
			FLOTE or spells *float*
			  correctly

Activities
  Concept sorts
  Alphabet songs
  Alphabet games
	Collect words for
	  Word Bank; sort
	  pictures for initial
	  consonants; some
	  analysis of final
	  consonants; some
	  analysis of consonant
	  blends and digraphs
		Study word families;
		  study short vowels
		  with picture and
		  word sorts
			Word sorts; word study
			  notebooks; study
			  long vowel patterns;
			  r-controlled vowels;
			  other vowel patterns

(based on Henderson, 1990, and adapted from Bear, 1991)

Emergent Readers and Preliterate Spelling

Children who cannot match written text with what they are saying are in the "preliterate" stage of spelling. This means that when they write, they use a blend of squiggles and recognizable letter forms that lacks a consistent sound-symbol correspondence between what they wrote and what they *say* they wrote.

Word Study: Preliterate Stage

Children's word study at this stage consists of such activities as learning the letter names of the alphabet, singing the alphabet song, matching uppercase and lowercase letters, and categorizing words and objects. Children do not learn many sight words until the next stage of development.

Beginning Readers and Early Letter-Name Spelling

Once children have acquired a rudimentary concept of word, they begin to collect a sight vocabulary. They can read a poem such as "Old Mister Rabbit" with some accuracy, in part because they are better at tracking print. These children are called beginning readers.

As shown in Figure 1, throughout this stage you will see the following reading behaviors:

- Children read aloud when they read to themselves.
- Children point to the words as they read.
- Children tend to read disfluently (Bear, 1989).

Given the synchrony of reading and spelling development, we can predict that these children are probably in either the "Early Letter-Name" or "Letter-Name" stage of spelling.

Harcourt Brace School Publishers

Early Letter-Name spellers usually choose logical beginning and final consonants for the sounds in the words they are trying to spell (Figure 1). Some spellings are based on how the words "feel" in their mouths when they say them (Read, 1975). Using this strategy, children in the Early Letter-Name stage often spell *dr* as *JR*. If you try saying these two digraphs yourself, you'll realize that this is a logical invention. The sounds /dr/ and /jr/ are articulated in nearly the same way. Also, children at this stage often omit vowels in their writing, except in important words like their own names.

Word Study: **Early Letter-Name Stage**
Children can sort their sight words by initial consonants. They enjoy hunting through familiar texts for words that begin with the same sound they are studying.

Beginning Readers and Letter-Name Spelling

In the early stages of beginning reading, children have a rudimentary concept of word. That is, if you ask them to find a particular word, they need to go back to the beginning of a line or to the beginning of the rhyme to find it. Children in the later stages of beginning reading are able to find the word without going back.

The difference in spelling between these two groups is quite remarkable. Children with a functional concept of word have progressed to the Letter-Name stage of spelling. This means that they continue to use a letter-name strategy to spell, but vowels have been added. Often they try to spell short vowel sounds based on the way the vowels feel in the mouth. For example, some children spell the short *e* in *bed* with the letter name *a* because the *a* feels that way in their mouths when they say it.

Children in the Letter-Name stage can sort known words based on the sound in the middle of the word. At first, children look at the similarities within families (*fat, cat, bat, rat*). After examining other short-vowel families, children begin to see the consonant-vowel-consonant (CVC) pattern. These children can generalize that the vowels in *cat, fan,* and even *ball* are all short *a*'s.

Word Study: **Letter-Name Stage**
Children are ready to learn about short-vowel families and the basic short-vowel patterns. However, long-vowel patterns should not be introduced because these spellers continue to use a single vowel to spell long vowels, for example, *cot* for *coat*.

Transitional Readers and Within-Word-Pattern Spelling

Toward the end of first grade, many children move to the next stage of literacy development. This is a transitional period in which children begin reading silently and generally need less support than beginning readers. Predictable text becomes less important, and as noted in the chart, easy chapter books are often chosen.

Given the synchrony of development, we see that transitional readers are in the Within-Word-Pattern stage of spelling (Bear, 1992). During this stage, children have learned to spell most short-vowel words and CVC patterns, and their invented spellings show them to be experimenting with long-vowel spelling patterns. They know enough about long- and short-vowel patterns to know that the word *coat* cannot be spelled *cot,* and they begin to use long-vowel patterns as they spell.

Word Study: **Transitional Stage**
Children examine long-vowel patterns for differences and similarities. They spend some time studying one vowel and its various patterns; for example, the CVVC pattern in *nail* and the CVCe pattern in *name*.

Writing in the Classroom

by Evelyn Cudd

Ms. Cudd is Third Grade Teacher, Rock Prairie School, College Station, Texas.

Q **I am confused about self-selected topics for writing. Is there ever a time when it's legitimate to assign a topic?**

A There is nothing pedagogically unsound about assigning a topic. In fact, research indicates that the most effective writing program is one that contains a mix of self-selected and assigned topics. What is unsound is just assigning a topic or handing children a story starter without discussion and planning. Remember also that within any assigned topic, there is usually an element of choice. If you ask children to write about a memorable moment in their lives, they choose the moment. Similarly, if children are writing about an endangered species, they choose the species and what aspect they wish to address.

Q **I've been hearing and reading a lot about product versus process. If I don't emphasize product, many of my children won't ever complete a piece. What's a proper balance?**

A Children need to understand the process that writers go through to bring a piece of writing to completion. Knowledge of this process alone, however, is not sufficient. Children must be expected to apply their knowledge to create their own published pieces. It is difficult to give an exact number, but I generally expect my children to publish one piece about every six weeks.

There's another aspect of the product issue. Process writing is only one part of an effective writing program. Children should be writing every day for a variety of purposes, such as note-taking, response journals, and learning logs. The writing done for these purposes is a product.

Children should also receive direct instruction in writing each day. These lessons can be minilessons or expanded lessons that are immediately applied to children's own writing. For instance, if you have a minilesson on sentence combining or expanding, a reasonable expectation would be for children to choose three or four sentences from their work and combine or expand them. This is a product. Most products are not full-process pieces.

Q **I have children who refuse to write. What can I do to get them to pick up a pencil and try?**

A One of the most effective ways to get children to write is by having them do written retellings of short, familiar folktales, fables, or simple books like *Caps for Sale.* Retellings remove the risk of failure and humiliation by allowing children to model good writing. These children often feel they have nothing to say and they know they have poor writing skills—frequently defined by teachers as spelling, handwriting, mechanics, and grammar. Because of past experiences, they are unwilling to chance ridicule or feel it is just too hard to write. When they retell a

Harcourt Brace School Publishers

story, they practice using the vocabulary, organization, and style of the model. Once children are writing, even "retold" writing, their confidence and fluency begin to increase.

The basic steps for retelling are

1. Read and discuss the selection.
2. Draw attention to the organization (what happened in the beginning, middle, ending) and effective word choice or special techniques like repetition.
3. Model a written retelling on the board or overhead.
4. Have children write their own version. This can be done collaboratively or individually.

Q **I know that process writing is important, but I don't want my children to have to take every piece of writing through all the stages. Is there one stage that shouldn't be skipped?**

A Prewriting is considered by many experts to be the most important stage of the writing process and the stage on which more of the writing time should be spent. The quality of children's writing that ensues is directly related to what goes on during this time. During this stage, children decide on purpose, form, and audience. They generate ideas about a topic and ways to organize those ideas. It is also a time for teacher modeling or collaborative compositions. Even if the writing goes no further, a great deal is learned about writing during this stage.

Q **What do I do with "hopeless" pieces that are only a few lines long and contain so many errors in syntax and mechanics that they are difficult to read and impossible to respond to in a positive way?**

A Research indicates that most responses to lower-level pieces are in the form of suggestions concerning spelling and mechanics. This should be avoided completely. It only discourages and further stifles any possibility for improvement in writing. Instead, focus on content. Ask questions about the piece that show an interest in the writer's thoughts. The power of personal interest and sincere questions should never be underestimated.

Q **Some authorities have recommended that handwriting no longer be taught. I feel that handwriting is important. What is your opinion?**

A The problem with formal instruction in handwriting is not the instruction itself, but the endless copying of specific writing exercises from the board or from dittos. This kind of practice inevitably leads to less time for meaningful writing, and its effect on letter formation and legibility is dubious.

It is important to demonstrate the correct formation of letters in manuscript and of cursive and letter connections if you are working with cursive. This can be accomplished in minilessons followed by short, guided practices. Once the letter formation has been learned, there is no justification for any handwriting practice as an end in itself.

Children should be taught that legibility is part of written communication. Opportunities for practicing handwriting should be accomplished through purposeful writing, not meaningless exercises.

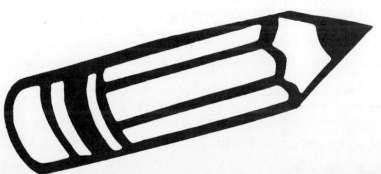

Prewriting Activities

Evelyn Cudd and others feel that prewriting is the most important step in the writing process. Here are some prewriting activities to add to your collection of tried-and-true favorites:

For Narrative and Creative Writing

- Draw.
- Brainstorm.
- Look through your journals.
- Visualize a scene.
- Go to the classroom Idea File.
- Fill in this diagram:

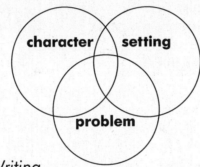

For Expository Writing

- Make a time line.
- Make a chart to record your data.
- Have a conference to narrow your topic.
- Fill in a planning chart:

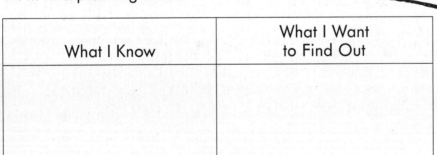

What I Know	What I Want to Find Out

- Fill in a chart that compares:

ME	A BIRD
can run	can run
can sing	can sing
can't fly	can fly

For Descriptive Writing

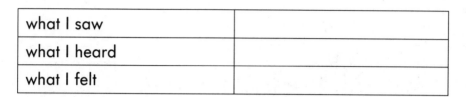

- Draw it.
- Talk about it.
- Move like the person, animal, or object.
- Make a chart that tells about it:

what I saw	
what I heard	
what I felt	

- Make a word web:

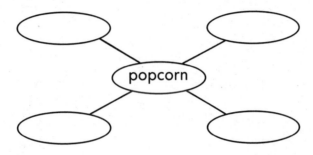

popcorn

What the teacher can provide
▲ daily scheduled time(s) for writing
▲ an "inspiration corner"
▲ a file box or bulletin board where everyone contributes ideas
▲ occasional guided imagery experiences for the whole group
▲ minilessons during small-group or individual conferences
▲ a role model of someone who writes to learn, writes for pleasure, writes to get things done

MAKING YOUR OWN BIG BOOKS

Big books lend themselves naturally to shared reading experiences because of their big type, simple and repetitive story text, and pictures large enough to see from the very back row. What a wonderful way to involve young children in the world of reading! Just as exciting are homemade big books, tangible proof to children that they are real authors who can create real books. These books will be the "best sellers" in your classroom, the ones that children of every ability level choose to read repeatedly.

Where to Begin

Making your own big books can be as simple or as involved as you want it to be. If you're making books that will be used all year, such as favorite nursery rhymes, songs, or folktales, you may want to use cardboard for the covers and heavy paper for the pages. (A laminating machine extends the life of any book.) Generally, using binder rings instead of staples or yarn to bind the book helps it last

longer. Remember, children can help you with all stages of bookmaking except using the laminating machine.

Big Book Possibilities

Consider making a big book when children

- write original stories.
- rewrite favorite stories.
- write a collection of poetry.
- record events for a class journal.
- write an attribute book, an alphabet book, or a counting book.
- record observations for a science log.

Harcourt Brace School Publishers

Binding Books

- Staple the cover and book pages together. Cover the staples with tape.

- Punch holes through the cover and the pages. Bind with metal rings or tie with yarn, ribbon, or shoelaces.

Types of Books

Shape Book   Draw a simple shape or copy a pattern for the shape from a coloring book or other source. Cut out enough copies of the shape to form the pages of a book.

Accordion Book   Reproduce four or more copies of a pattern, and tape the pages together. Fold the book accordion-style to close it.

Pocket Book   Form a pocket using a large sheet of construction paper or a large manila envelope. Tape the pocket to the back of a pattern. Children's writing can be stored inside the pocket.

Trifold Book   Reproduce three copies of a pattern, and tape them together along the sides. Fold in the right side and then the left. The writing or the drawing is found inside.

Flap Book   Reproduce one copy of a pattern. Attach a construction-paper flap as a cover with children's writing papers attached to the top of the pattern. Lift the pages to read.

Double-Hinged Book   Use a pattern that can be cut down the center. Make two copies of the pattern, and cut one of the patterns down the center. Hinge each side, and attach children's writing inside.

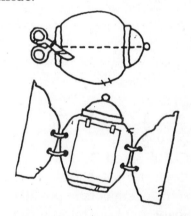

Clothesline Book   Reproduce copies of a pattern for children to draw or write on. Display the writing along a clothesline.

Door or Window Book

Use a pattern for a building, such as a house, a store, a dollhouse, or a barn. Make two copies of the pattern. Cut out three sides of a large door or a window in the center of one of the patterns. Then staple the two patterns together with the door or window cutout on top. Fold back the door or window, and outline the area that can be seen when it is opened. In that space, have children help you write a short song, nursery rhyme, or poem.

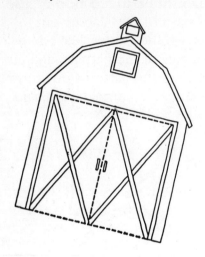

Child-Sized Books Don't forget to make smaller versions of especially popular shape books. Children can use these as journals, or they can draw and write their own version of a story to take home and share with family members.

Storing Big Books

1. Suspend a metal rod from the ceiling or use a clothing rack. Clip each big book to a skirt hanger, and hang it on the rod.

2. Store big books in large, plastic zip-type bags, available from school supply stores. Hang the bags on a rod.

3. Store big books inside large cartons. Label the outside of the box with the titles.

Sharing Big Books

Children will be proud to share the big books they produce. Consider sharing in these ways:

- Read aloud in small groups.
- Read independently or with a partner.
- Share with classroom visitors.
- Display in the school library.
- Give as a gift.
- "Rent out" to share with family members.

Harcourt Brace School Publishers

Classroom
Management

"**T**eachers . . . are always thinking about what their children know and how to help them grow from that point."

→ Sandra Wilde

Integrating Instruction

by Patricia Smith

During a nighttime theme suggested by one of the children, a class of first graders is exploring the need all animals have for periods of sleep. While engaged in this theme, children hear a personal narrative and read two fiction selections, at least four poems, and a set of directions. These literary experiences launch further research into sleep patterns of animals and linkages to science content on formation of shadows. Children write their own poems about sleep and read additional literature about sleeping.

These children are learning to read, write, speak, and listen through a thematic unit that is rich in

- quality literature
- cross-curricular connections
- opportunities for direct instruction in reading and writing strategies
- varied grouping options
- important concepts

Benefits for Children

- Connections are formed in the brain.
- Skills are learned in a meaningful context.
- Vocabulary and concepts are developed and solidified through repeated usage over time.
- Choices within the unit offer children ownership of their learning.
- Opportunities for learning within a community are plentiful.
- Learning time is maximized when multiple subjects are integrated.
- Opportunities exist for motivating learners through the topic, literature, and learning experiences.

Harcourt Brace School Publishers

with Themes

Organizing Themes Within the Classroom

Organizational Pattern	Example	Content
Topic	Environment	Literature and experiences about environment
Concept	Improving the World	Literature and experiences about improving the world
Genre	Biographies	Biographies and experiences to learn about a variety of people
Author	Pat Hutchins	Literature and experiences to explore books by Pat Hutchins

Harcourt Brace School Publishers

Planning for thematic instruction

- Determine a broad theme that will support many connections.
- Determine process and content objectives.
- Determine how much time will be allotted, keeping in mind the need for flexibility to allow for children's interests and needs.
- Determine resources.
  - Literature
  - Reference materials
  - Audiovisual materials
  - Artifacts, some of which could come from children
  - Expert guest speakers
- Determine learning experiences.

Learning Experiences Within a Theme

Type	Purpose
Initiating	Motivates Activates background knowledge Sets the focus
Ongoing	Engages the learner in authentic reading, writing, listening, and speaking
Culminating	Summarizes Synthesizes Determines direction for further learning

- Determine which learning experiences will be conducted independently, with partners, in small cooperative groups, or with the whole class.
- Determine the evaluation measures for inclusion in children's portfolios.

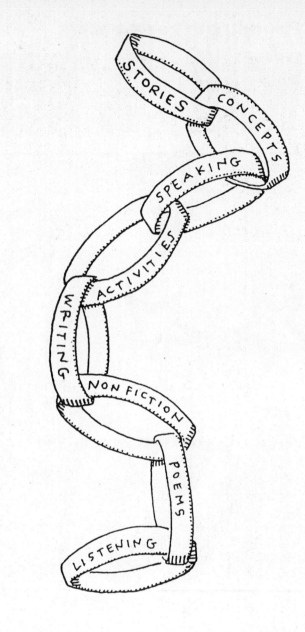

PORTFOLIO POSSIBILITIES	
Portfolio Entry	**Produced by**
Learning logs	Child
Reading/writing logs	Child
Work samples	Child
Culminating product	Child
Self-evaluations	Child
Observational checklists	Teacher
Group evaluation forms	Peers

Harcourt Brace School Publishers

Principles to keep in mind

Does my thematic unit

____ contain quality fiction and nonfiction?

____ provide material on a variety of reading levels?

____ offer opportunities for authentic reading, writing, listening, and speaking?

____ further the development of strategic readers and writers?

____ form natural links to other curriculum areas?

____ offer opportunities for choice?

____ provide opportunities for children to learn in a community of learners?

____ promote inquiry into new information?

Planning Tip: Steps in promoting inquiry into new information

1. Complete the shared literature experiences chosen to initiate the unit.
2. Use a K-W-L chart to determine what children know and what they want to know about the topic.
3. Form groups of children with a shared interest to explore the questions listed in the W column of the K-W-L chart.
4. Support the research efforts of children.
5. Encourage daily small-group and self-evaluations on the progress of the inquiry and collaboration efforts.
6. Arrange for the sharing of information learned.
7. Promote active listening by the class so that new information can be added to the L column of the K-W-L chart.
8. Help children determine future inquiries for self-directed learning of this topic.

Planning Tip: Working with other teachers

Post a large planning chart like the one below. Encourage teachers to use self-stick notes to add to the "Resources" and "Learning Experiences" sections. After sufficient time for input, meet with other teachers to select and sequence ideas for the thematic unit. You will find that even teachers not directly involved in the unit may have resources and ideas to suggest.

PLANNING CHART	
Theme:	Time Frame:
Content and Process Objectives:	
Resources:	
Learning Experiences:	
Evaluation Measures:	

Harcourt Brace School Publishers

Managing Learning Centers

by Judy Giglio

Learning centers—self-contained spaces for investigations in particular content areas—promote independence, responsibility, and cooperative behavior. When children understand what is expected of them, learning centers are a perfect match for their learning style and natural curiosity. Managing the flow of children and materials in and out of centers and continually assessing the learning that is taking place are big parts of a primary teacher's job.

Planning is the key to successful centers.

Plan for and with children. Keep your expectations high, but realistic.

Have all the materials in the center labeled in advance and ready to use.

Set aside time to introduce and explain all center activities. Demonstrate the use of unfamiliar materials.

Arrange your room to accommodate whole-group, small-group, and individual activities.

Enlist children's help in managing the centers.

With children, establish guidelines for behavior in the centers.

Decide on the number of children permitted in each center at any one time. Do this by displaying the number or by providing a limited number of name tags for children to wear while in the center.

Display a sign-up sheet at each center. This will tell you at a glance who is doing what. Check the sign-up sheets regularly to see if some children always use the same center.

Set a time for working in centers.

Evaluation of center activities should be an ongoing process.

Observe children in the centers, watching for those who are not sure what to do or are having trouble getting started.

As you confer with individuals or work with small groups, keep an eye and ear open for what is happening elsewhere.

Review with children what they have accomplished in the centers. Change those activities that don't seem to work.

Two Approaches to Classroom Management

If you're new to the idea of learning centers, consider introducing just one or two at a time. Here are two different approaches.

Content-Area Learning Centers

Some teachers establish learning centers that cover all the areas of the curriculum. The materials and activities in the centers change continuously, depending on the themes children are exploring. (See the planning chart below.)

Figure 1: Sample Planning Chart

Theme: **Westward Ho!**
Dates: **January 12–21**

Whole-Group Activities

1. Introduce the theme with photographs and a shared reading of the book *Gila Monsters Meet You at the Airport* by Marjorie Sharmat (Macmillan), with written responses.
2. Western Clothing Day
3. Cooking on the trail
4. Jobs on a ranch
5. Country line dancing
6. Making graphs about plants and animals of the desert

BULLETIN BOARD: Western characters to be used for storytelling

FIELD TRIP: Visit a local riding stable, and record experiences in a journal.

Learning Center Activities

LANGUAGE ARTS: Categorize Western words, match words and pictures, play a game: Gila Monsters at the Airport.

WRITING: Make shape books.

SCIENCE: Read and write about animals of the West.

SOCIAL STUDIES: Role-play jobs on a ranch, make Conestoga wagons, read maps.

MATH: Weigh gold, make a picture.

ART: Follow directions for sand painting.

DRAMATIC PLAY: Create a western campsite.

MUSIC: Learn folk songs.

READING CORNER: Theme books for quiet reading and take-home reading

Harcourt Brace School Publishers

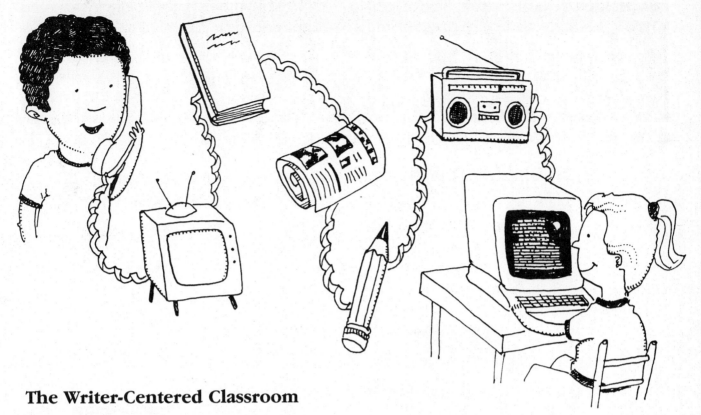

The Writer-Centered Classroom

Instruction is geared toward the individual child in a writer-centered classroom. The teacher serves as a facilitator who provides encouragement and feedback. The day begins with a whole-class meeting in which each child reports on a current writing project. It's a time for the teacher to determine where each child is and to plan instruction and guidance. Individual conferences are held with some children while others are busy working. The teacher provides minilessons on a process or skill that the whole group or a small group may need. Topics for lessons are tied to children's needs, as well as to the core curriculum. The following work areas could be included in such a classroom:

Independent study area (tables, chairs, books)

Writing area (all sorts of paper and writing supplies, bookmaking supplies, typewriter, computer)

Art area (variety of art supplies, easels)

Library area (books of all kinds, flannel board, character puppets, puppets and stage, system for children to borrow books for take-home use)

Research area (books, magazines, dictionaries, globe, maps, posters, science displays)

Group meeting area (large rug, Author's Chair)

Portfolio area (storage and easy access to children's portfolios)

In a writer-centered classroom, children rotate through the different work areas throughout the day. During a Westward Ho! theme, for example, children may be involved in writing stories, recording information in a science log, learning how to do research or read a map, listening to a tall tale, or painting a mural in response to a shared reading.

INTEGRATING

by Dr. Shelley B. Wepner and **Dr. Nancy E. Seminoff**

Assistant to the Dean, School of Education
William Patterson College
Wayne, New Jersey

Dean, School of Education
William Patterson College
Wayne, New Jersey

Harcourt Brace School Publishers

TECHNOLOGY

Young children of the nineties do not have to go very far to experience the excitement of "the magic kingdom." Software for primary children dazzles the senses as different constructs, strategies, and materials are used to promote literacy. Although debates abound about the place of technological "edutainment" in primary classrooms, technology certainly can contribute to children's literacy development if it is considered part of good curriculum planning. In creating these plans, we need to consider the concepts and content that we want children to acquire, the materials we will use, and the organization of activities. These three considerations determine how we will choose software and how we will organize our classrooms and our time.

SOFTWARE

In selecting software, consider these suggestions:

- Select software that supports your philosophy and methods for developing literacy. If you use trade books to teach reading, consider the Living Books collection (by Brøderbund) in which the entire contents of popular books such as *Dr. Seuss's ABC, The Berenstain Bears Get in a Fight,* and *The Tortoise and the Hare* appear to come alive on the screen. If you use phonics, consider *Reader Rabbit's Interactive Reading Journey,* which features a reading kingdom of "letterlands" with short, instructional stories about the main character, Sam the Lion, and his animal friends.

- Select software that supports learning about your topical units or thematic units. For example, animals are a favorite topic of children in the primary grades. Three software products that support a unit on animals are

  1 the Explore-A-Science Series (by William K. Bradford), which includes three separate packages entitled *Dinosaurs, Whales,* and *Wolves;*

  2 the Learn About Series (by Wings for Learning/Sunburst), which includes two packages, *Learn About Insects* and *Learn About Animals;* and

  3 *Zoo Keeper* (by Davidson & Associates), which is a learning adventure in which children help save the animals in the zoo.

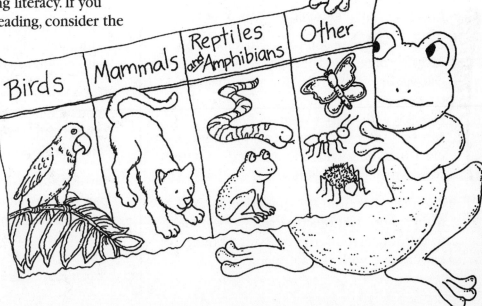

Birds   Mammals   Reptiles and Amphibians   Other

- Identify age-appropriate software that allows children to write about their units of study. For example, *Kid Works 2* (by Davidson & Associates) offers a word processor, a paint program, and text-to-speech capabilities so that children can create, illustrate, and listen to their writing. *Make-A-Book* (by Teacher Support Software) offers an easy-to-use word processor that prints children's writing in book form.

- Provide software that promotes the exploration of information, particularly for topical or thematic units. For example, two CD-ROM encyclopedias, *My First Encyclopedia* (by Knowledge Adventure) and *Random House Kid's Encyclopedia,* enable children to browse with ease and meander through information in both a linear and nonlinear way. Children on video, known as "VidKids," talk children through these programs as they explore and manipulate information through a variety of activities.

- Think of ways to combine packages to support your instructional focus. For example, if you use author studies to help children focus on one author at a time, the Living Books collection includes two of Mercer Mayer's books, *Just Grandma and Me* and *Little Monster at School,* and two of Marc Brown's books, *Arthur's Teacher Trouble* and *Arthur's Birthday,* that children can study in depth.

- Look for software companies that focus on early learning. One company, Edmark, has specialized in early learning for more than twenty years. As a consequence, *Bailey's Book House*® and *Trudy's Time and Place House*™ offer enchanting environments for exploring the sounds and meanings of letters, words, rhymes, and stories.

- Use materials from the documentation from school editions (the teacher's guide) to introduce, reinforce, or extend children's experience with the software.

- Become sufficiently familiar with the package so that you know whether it is most appropriate for an initial introduction to a whole group, a small group, or an individual student, and whether it lends itself to teacher-child collaboration or child-child collaboration.

ORGANIZING YOUR CLASSROOM

Even with only one computer in your classroom, you have many ways to integrate technology successfully:

- Try to arrange for the use of projection devices such as large-screen monitors and LCD (Liquid Crystal Display) panels so that a large group of children can watch one large monitor.

- Discipline yourself to acquire in-depth knowledge of the software so that you know how to schedule activities to make maximum use of available time.

- Create a daily and weekly schedule to ensure equitable use.

- Create systems that enable children to use software on their own or in cooperative learning groups. Pair two to four children at a time for programs and ongoing projects that lend themselves to group work. Find out ahead of time which children are comfortable with the computer so that they can be paired with children who are less proficient.

- Use a learning-center approach so that while some children are working on a computer project, other children are working on a different project.

- Involve parents. At Back-to-School night, ask parents to volunteer to work with children in the classroom on software activities. A parent can be particularly helpful when the software calls for teacher-child collaboration (Wepner & Seminoff, 1994).

Harcourt Brace School Publishers

- Identify someone in your building or district who can help troubleshoot to ensure that instructional plans flow smoothly.

Even as you manage with one computer, consider these suggestions to expand hardware availability:

- Bargain with other teachers to borrow additional computers for a specified period of time.

- Identify other locations in the community or school where computers are available for students to use on their own time.

- Look to corporations for donations of their "obsolete" machines whenever they are upgrading to newer platforms.

- Have PTAs and other groups involved with the school look for ways to secure additional hardware and software through grants and philanthropic organizations.

AND MORE . . .

- Use word processing, graphics, and desktop publishing programs to communicate to children's families, through newsletters or one-page updates, about what children are learning and how computers are helping. Use some of the same software packages to create classroom posters, bulletin boards, and instructional activities.

- Attend local, statewide, and national computer-oriented conferences, or attend technology-related workshops at other conferences.

- Subscribe to technology magazines and journals such as *Technology and Learning* (330 Progress Road, Dayton, OH 45449) and *The Computing Teacher* (International Society for Technology in Education, 1787 Agate Street, Eugene, OR 97403-1923).

As one teacher colleague, Ms. Elsie Nigohosian, said when she began to integrate technology into her kindergarten curriculum, "Good-bye, Saturdays!" Initially skittish about taking the plunge, she discovered that even her typically dysfunctional children were captivated by the on-screen activities, often requesting time away from recess to work on the computer (Wepner & Seminoff, 1994). With a little help from your colleagues, weekend forays into software reviews are not necessary for the pleasure of seeing your children's animated faces. 🍎

Making Flexible Grouping Work for You

by Dr. Marguerite Cogorno Radencich
University of South Florida, Tampa, Florida

◆ What does flexible grouping really mean?

Flexible grouping is temporary grouping that varies according to instructional goals as well as children's needs and interests. It can be seen as a "cafeteria" of options that includes whole-group instruction, teacher-facilitated small groups, cooperative groups, pairs, and individual work. In a cafeteria, you wouldn't want to select just one part of the food pyramid. So, too, do you need a balanced diet with your grouping.

◆ How do I start?

Think about the kinds of groups you now use. Then plan to gradually add one more type of group to your "tray." Talk with or visit colleagues who use types of grouping that you are interested in trying.

Begin the new type of grouping with an easy activity so that children are not trying to learn a new organizational system and new content at the same time. For example, children can ease into group work by showing books to each other, telling each other about their artwork, and reading or pretend-reading their writing to each other. Gradually, you can release responsibility to children, who can check off a task when they complete it and self-evaluate their group behavior with a smiley face, straight face, or sad face.

◆ I'm trying to find time for flexible grouping, but my whole-class instruction tends to use up my language arts period.

HELP!

This situation is not uncommon. You might want to schedule groups early in the period to be sure you get to them. The problem may be, however, that you do not trust your children in groups. One teacher I know was able by the second semester of first grade to have pairs work together with an easy book. She did this by (1) listing on a chart a series of daily activities around the books, such as "your side–my side" reading, games with sight words from the books, and cutting up and reassembling a sentence from the book, (2) taking the whole class through this series of activities, and (3) having the class work through the series in groups while she supervised. Only then did she feel ready to start having groups work independently while the rest of the class worked on the series of activities. You would see pairs go to the chart and point to their next task.

If you are unable to schedule small groups, consider the reason, share my suggestions with colleagues, and develop a plan that will work for you.

◆ **How can I organize my schedule for flexible grouping? I want to make sure I'm keeping all children on task and learning, without losing my sanity in the process.**

Following are tips from teachers who have become comfortable with flexible grouping:

TIP Keep a chart of your learning centers and activities. The chart might have a designated number of spaces next to each center, to represent the maximum number of children who can work there. You might also use laminated shapes made by each child, with the child's name on his or her shape. These can be attached to a laminated chart with sticky tabs or rolled masking tape. This strategy works well if you previously make some or all of the center selections. If children are to make all of the selections, you would have a whole class clustering around the chart simultaneously. In the latter case, you might want to cut apart the rows for the centers and use each as a label on which children place their name shapes.

Other possibilities might be a kitchen center, a dress-up center, and simulation centers such as a post office, a restaurant, or a travel agency. Or, you may wish to list activities

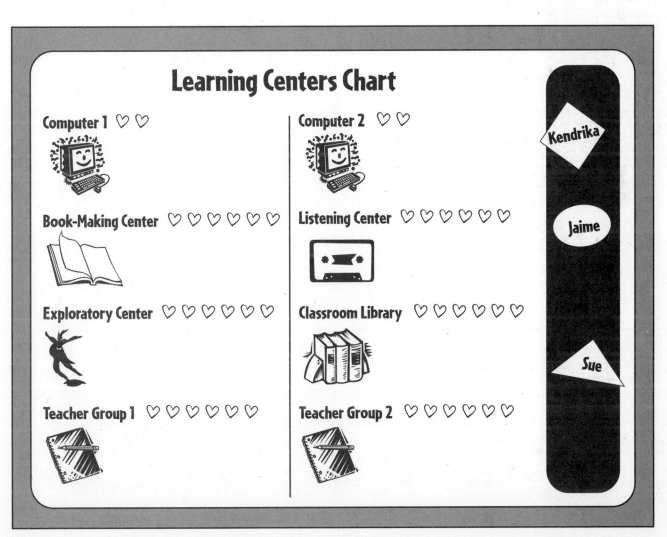

Harcourt Brace School Publishers

rather than centers. Activities might include buddy reading, sharing of writing, listening to a story, and acting out a story.

TIP As an alternative to the above, use a book display rack to label each center or activity in the classroom. Children's name cards can be placed in the spaces for designated centers or activities. A designated reader can inform the class of their placements. If you preselect centers or activities, another time can be allowed for student self-selection.

TIP Think about which of your activities you might try in each group format. There is no one right type of group for each instructional goal, but the following checklist gives some examples.

TIP Involve children in ongoing projects. This has several advantages. Ongoing projects tend to be engaging. Children will know that they can come back to unfinished projects at a later time. And you will be trading off time in creating daily assignments for less-frequent, although more in-depth, planning.

◆ **How can I meet the needs of less-proficient readers without resorting to ability grouping? What are my options?**

The term ability grouping should perhaps be changed to proficiency grouping because the question is not one of innate ability but of proficiency attained. Proficiency groups have

Matching Activities to Grouping Options

	Whole Class	Teacher-Facilitated Small Groups	Cooperative Groups	Pairs	Individuals
Teacher Read-Aloud	√	√			
Demonstrations	√	√			
Choral Reading/Echo Reading	√	√			
Readers Theatre/Story Theater	√	√			
Rereading with Taped Story				√	√
Buddy Reading				√	
Support for Emergent or Struggling Readers		√			
Journals	√			√	√
Literature Circles			√		
Self-Selected Reading				√	√
Projects	√		√	√	√
Conferencing				√	√
Direct Instruction	√	√			
Author's Chair	√		√		
Learning Centers			√	√	√

Harcourt Brace School Publishers

Children working in heterogeneous cooperative groups learn to draw on each other's strengths. Some may be better readers or writers, but others may be especially creative, have a knack for organizational details, have knowledge to share in an area of special interest, or just have lots of good ideas! Encourage children of all ages and ability levels to share their questions, knowledge, ideas, and strategies, whether in whole-class activities, small groups, or partner interactions.

a definite place within flexible grouping. But we are not talking here about static groups of redbirds, bluebirds, and buzzards. Teachers who use flexible grouping may work with less-proficient readers as a group, daily if necessary, and invite visitors to the group on occasion. However, this will not be the only kind of group in which less-proficient readers interact. At times you may blend them into skill groups with some of the other children to work on a commonly needed skill. There may well be cooperative learning and peer tutoring in which children help one another. And there will be interest groups. With a variety of groups, you will be eliminating some of the problems with traditional ability grouping, such as low expectations that result in fewer high-level questions, less wait time, and less practice with reading itself. 🍎

MULTI-AGE CLASSROOMS

◆ I teach in a K–2 mixed-grade class. Do you have any flexible grouping suggestions for me?

Grouping options available to all teachers may, of course, be used in multi-age classes. Many teachers who teach multi-grade classes in a pod also find it helpful to regroup children for some degree of homogeneity during language arts and math instruction. In a K–2 combination, this might result in K–1 and 1–2 groups. Whether regrouping is possible for you or not, you always have the makings for good peer tutoring. Be careful, though, not to overuse stronger children as tutors. They, too, need your instruction.

A CONVERSATION WITH DR. SANDRA WILDE ABOUT MINILESSONS

Sandra Wilde, Associate Professor, School of Education, Portland State University, and the author of *You Kan Red This! Spelling and Punctuation for Whole Language Classrooms, K–6* (Heinemann, 1992), has used minilessons to explore the role of instruction in a child-centered spelling curriculum. In this conversation, she gives examples of how teachers might use minilessons across the language arts curriculum.

Q What exactly is a minilesson?

 I love the idea of minilessons because they're a way for teachers to think of instruction as a brief, focused adjunct to a child-centered curriculum. A minilesson is a short, usually teacher-directed explanation or exploration of a single topic. Teachers choose topics for minilessons by being kid watchers (Yetta Goodman's term) who are always thinking about what their children know and how to help them grow from that point.

Q Where did you get the idea of minilessons?

 From Lucy Calkins's *Art of Teaching Writing* (Heinemann, 1986). She suggests that teachers not be "afraid to teach," but that teaching is a small piece of a writing workshop classroom rather than the major source of children's developing knowledge and strategies.

Q Can you take us through the process of developing and teaching a minilesson about spelling?

 There's one I've done several times with primary-grade children whose invented spelling shows that they've discovered that the /k/ sound is spelled with *c* in some words (like *cat*) and with *k* in others (like *kite*). I ask them to think of all the words they can that start with this sound, which I then list on the board, grouped according to beginning letter. I then ask them what they notice. For younger writers, being aware that we have more than one way to spell the same sound is about all the generalization they can handle. With more sophisticated children—many second and third graders—I can ask them to think about why some words start with *c* and some with *k*.

Q How does this fit into the bigger picture?

 My purpose is to draw on the children's existing knowledge about how words are spelled and then encourage them to develop hypotheses that will extend their understanding a little. I don't follow it with any exercise, because my purpose has been fulfilled by the minilesson itself. I will usually, however, encourage them to look for words starting with /k/ in their reading and to add any new ones to the list for as long as it remains on the board.

Q Do children like minilessons?

A It's always exciting for me to see that children are interested even in topics like spelling that seem dull to adults, if instruction is geared to their level of development and pushes them to think.

Q What are some other possible topics for minilessons in reading and language arts?

A Here are a few. With first graders who are beginning to explore picture dictionaries, encourage children to browse in the dictionaries and then ask for their ideas about how to get to the right part of the dictionary if they know what the first letter of a word is. Your role is to integrate their own ideas into an easy and sensible strategy. (For example, "Look at the alphabet chart to see about how far into the dictionary the word will be.")

If your children are showing some interest in learning about quotation marks, put a comic strip on the overhead and show how it could be converted into a story with dialogue carriers and quotation marks to indicate who's talking and what they're saying.

Ask children to list two kinds of books they've read: those about events that really happened and those that could have happened but didn't. After discussing how children knew the difference, you can use the terms *nonfiction* and *fiction* to label the concepts.

In preparation for children publishing their own books, ask them to look at the title page, copyright page, and dedication page of "real" books as you explain what information is there and why.

Q How can a teacher best fit minilessons into the school day?

A There are a number of ways. A daily reading or writing workshop can begin with a minilesson. You can pull together a small group of children who seem ready to explore a particular area. Also, attentive kid watching during reading and writing conferences will provide many opportunities for one-on-one "teachable moment" minilessons.

Q What do you like best about minilessons?

A Two things: the opportunity for the teacher to be directly responsive to children's needs, and the enthusiasm of children when instruction is focused and interactive.

"A daily reading or writing workshop can begin with a minilesson."

Smooth Transitions

Transitions—from place to place, from whole-group to independent activities, from time period to time period, from teacher to teacher— are difficult for young learners. Here are some teacher-tested ideas for making the most of those in-between moments that are part of every school day.

Riddles and Word Games

When children have to wait for someone or something at school, keep them busy thinking! Adapt any of these oral language activities and see how quickly time flies!

WHAT IF? Ask questions such as the following; then encourage children to make up their own questions for the group.

- What might happen if there weren't any numbers at school?
- What might happen if the sun stopped shining?
- What might happen if the Three Little Pigs met the Three Bears?
- What might happen if fish could talk?

NAME GAMES Give children riddles about their names; then encourage them to take a turn.

- I'm thinking of someone's first name that rhymes with _____.
- I'm thinking of someone's first name that starts with the same sound as _____.
- I'm thinking of two children's last names that both end with _____.

WHAT WOULD YOU DO? Present problems such as the following and have several children suggest solutions. Some children may want to make up their own problems.

- We're playing a game, but I never get a turn. What can I do?
- My friend fell down and hurt himself. What can I do?
- I'm reading a book. I don't know some of the words. What can I do?

Encouraging Independence

During planning time, make a distinction between those things that are *musts* (everyone must do them) and those that are *choices*. Always have plenty of activity choices available so that children can never say they have "nothing to do."

Harcourt Brace School Publishers

Immediately after children have moved into various independent activities, circulate among them to see that they are refocused before you begin to work with small groups or individuals. Providing time for children to "settle in" to new activities supports independence.

At the end of an activity period, occasionally take time to discuss the overall conduct of the group. Have children tell what they accomplished. Talk about the things that seemed to go well and those that didn't. Involve the children in making suggestions for change.

After giving instructions for an activity, have one or two children repeat the instructions as they understand them. This will help to clear up misunderstandings in advance and help avoid interruptions during independent activity time.

Managing Centers

For children who have had little experience working independently, you may wish to organize independent time so that they rotate, in small groups, through a sequence of activities. Use a chart such as the following. The composition of groups and center activities may change each week.

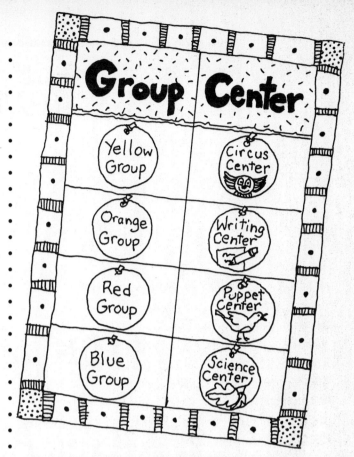

For especially popular centers, you may need to post sign-up sheets. Establish a routine so that children know when they may write their name on *one* of the lists. Encourage children to be responsible for telling the next person on the list that they are done and that space is now available in the center.

Harcourt Brace School Publishers

JOURNALING:

A CONVERSATION WITH DR. DONNA OGLE

Donna Ogle is Chair of the

Reading and Language Arts

Department at National-Louis

University in Evanston, Illinois.

Harcourt Brace School Publishers

Write from the start! Make journals a habit in your classroom and enjoy finding out what your children know and are interested in. When you encourage children to compose their own thoughts in personal journals, they develop interest in written language and learn to engage in reflective thinking. Journals are often a favorite text from which children choose to read. They can also become a major part of a primary integrated curriculum. In a hands-on science program, journals might be the place where children record their predictions and observations.

The advantages of journals are many. Yet teachers often wonder how to get started using them and whether they are worth the time for primary children.

Q **How do I get started?**

A Construct individual journals for children with primary paper that has space for drawing and writing. Write, or have children write, their names on the covers and then let them illustrate the covers. One teacher made journals a family affair by asking family members to design covers for blank journals when they came for an initial parents' night. When children received their journals with drawings and messages from their parents, the whole purpose of journaling was clear and the joy immediate!

Q **How do the youngest children write in their journals?**

A Even when they start kindergarten, many children bring with them the ability to write some words, especially their names. Find out what they can write by asking them to write all the words they know in their journals. Or ask them to write about what they want to learn in school or about favorite animals, foods, TV shows, and so on.

Children can draw responses to these queries even if they can't write the individual words. As children draw, you can circulate with small slips of paper to write the full messages children want. Give them the slips of paper to paste in their journals. In this way you will have a permanent record of children's intended writing.

Many primary children find writing to be slow and laborious. Help these children enjoy journaling by encouraging them to construct entries in other ways. They can share ideas by drawing pictures of what they think is important. They can cut out text and illustrations from magazines that help communicate their ideas and then paste these in their journals. When you create class messages and news updates, make copies for children to include in their journals. Some of the most creative and useful journals I've seen in primary grades were created from a variety of media.

Harcourt Brace School Publishers

Q **How can I help children use the journal productively?**

A Some teachers like to provide time at the end of the day for writing in a group journal. By bringing the children together and asking them to think about the day's events, you nurture the habit of reflection. Write children's contributions in the class journal, including their names by what they said.

One teacher noted a dramatic difference in her children when she used group journaling. They took more notice of what the class was doing. At an open house, several parents seemed particularly surprised and pleased. One explained, "When we ask Sara what happens in school, she now can tell us specific events. Before, she would just shrug and tell us she couldn't remember."

Q **How often should children write in their journals?**

A If daily journaling seems like too much, then take time once or twice a week to reflect with the group. Sometimes a group discussion can stimulate children to return to their desks and write. Each teacher needs to find what works best for a particular group. You can try alternating a day of group journaling with a day of individual journaling. Remember that when journals are kept at their desks, children are more likely to use them. Since some will "take to" journaling more than others, encourage this approach.

Q **What kinds of things should children write in their journals?**

A This is up to you and the children. In some classrooms, journals are for personal reflection only. But journals are also certainly appropriate for content learning ("writing to know"), especially in science. They are also a useful place for children to record responses to literature.

Q **Should teachers respond in children's journals?**

A This depends on the kind of journaling you want to use. Dialogue journals are valuable additions to your literature program. Children reading independently can use the journal as a way of sharing with you their responses to what they read. You can further understand children's involvement with a story by exploring their comments and asking probing questions.

Harcourt Brace School Publishers

Pacing Literacy Instruction:
An Interview with Dr. W. Dorsey Hammond

Dr. Hammond, Professor of Education at Oakland University in Rochester, Michigan, answers some questions teachers often ask about the pacing of instruction.

Q **I often wonder if my pacing of instruction is appropriate. Are there some basic guidelines I can use?**

A Pacing of instruction is something we must constantly monitor. Every thoughtful teacher wonders about it. "Am I moving the instruction too quickly or too slowly?" "Am I trying to do too much?" "Am I leaving out some important skills or strategies?" and so on.

Only the individual teacher can make these decisions. The basic guideline is that our children must be involved in learning experiences that are challenging enough for new learning to occur but not so difficult that children are overwhelmed and begin to be afraid or withdraw. Conversely, the material and learning experiences must not be so easy that children aren't learning anything new and become bored. Reading teachers think about the appropriate match between learners and the learning activities as the "instructional level," or "range."

Q **I am using a program that provides several activities and lessons for each selection in the children's literature anthology. Do I have to do everything?**

A The key here is to be selective. There won't be time for you to do everything. Nor is it necessary. You may decide, for example, to omit certain activities or even to be selective in the stories the children read.

Q **Why are there so many activities and stories if I'm not expected to do them all?**

A So you will have choice. Just as when you go into a library, a bookstore, or even a grocery store, you choose what you want and need or what your children want and need. This is not to suggest that you should skip too much—it is just that you can make informed decisions.

Q **If I skip a story in the anthology, won't the children miss out on some of the skills?**

A All of the stories in a carefully planned literature program are worth reading, and each contributes to your children's reading growth. However, the skills and strategies are so carefully interwoven and repeated throughout the fabric of the entire program that you can comfortably be a bit selective.

In addition to choosing *what* your children read, you will need to make some decisions about *how* they read. You will choose to have children read some selections with your guidance and direction so that you can model good reading strategies. Other selections may be read independently by all children or by a portion of your class. Still other selections may be read and discussed by a literature circle or other subgroup of your class.

Q You mentioned grouping. I have a wide range of reading abilities in my classroom. Should I have reading groups in different books?

A This is really a district or individual school decision made at the local level. Research tells us that children in the "low group" seldom grow or achieve well enough to get out of the low group. Students really do need opportunities to work with others who are at different achievement levels.

Q I never seem to have enough time to do all I want to do. Do you have any recommendations?

A Really good teachers are always saying, "If I just had more time." It is part of our profession. It seems we are always adding something to the curriculum but never taking anything out.

Here are three things we can do to save time and increase our efficiency:

1. Think about a school day and ask yourself, "What did we do today that didn't seem to make a difference?" Do this for a few days, and you will probably find some activities that aren't worth the time you spend on them. In other words, clean up your school day and throw out what isn't needed.

2. Establish with students rituals of getting underway, moving from one activity to another, settling down in the morning or after lunch, taking out and putting away materials, and so on. As we find 30 seconds here and 30 seconds there, it soon adds up to a few minutes a day that can be used to read a few extra pages to your students or allow them to read or write for a few more minutes.

3. Look for activities that increase student interaction, such as cooperative learning. Have students read to one another in small groups rather than having one student read and twenty-five students listen. Involve students in choral and echo reading. Allow students to help one another and explain things to one another, thus reinforcing and promoting language interaction.

Finally, accept that the pacing of instruction will always be an issue with many dimensions. There is no one prescription. Trust your own judgment and the judgment of your colleagues.

Harcourt Brace School Publishers

Meeting Individual Needs

"Almost all children can learn to read and write, and they really want to."

→ Dr. Barbara Bowen Coulter

Learning Styles/Multiple Intelligences:
What They Are & What to Do About Them

by Guy Blackburn, Ph.D.

Dr. Blackburn is Director of Staff Development, Oakland Schools, Waterford, Michigan.

Teachers have always known that children learn at different rates and in different ways. Skillful teachers adapt their teaching techniques and learning activities to respond to these apparent differences. In recent years, learning theorists have further refined our ideas about learning, providing teachers with exciting new ways to plan, organize, and assess what goes on in their classrooms.

Two such approaches are "learning styles or learning modalities," as presented in the work of Rita Dunn and Bernice McCarthy, and Howard Gardner's theory of multiple intelligences. These theories focus on what occurs in a learner's mind as he or she undertakes a task or attempts to learn something. Following are suggestions and formats for practical applications of each theory.

Learning styles

For years, Rita Dunn has encouraged teachers to alter instruction to match the learning styles of children. She also points out that teachers have preferred styles and that the happiest match occurs when the teacher's style and the child's style match. This is probably impossible when there are 25–30 children in a classroom. So it is imperative, according to Dunn, that teachers systematically screen children and adjust teaching and learning experiences—*as much as possible*—to children's learning styles or modalities. The major modes or styles are

- **Visual** These learners learn more easily when they see things.
- **Auditory** These learners acquire knowledge more readily through listening.
- **Verbal** These children prefer to learn through talking and expressing their thoughts in writing.
- **Tactile/Kinesthetic** These children tend to learn best by touching things and manipulating concrete objects.
- **Smell and taste** Although these modalities of learning are restricted by practical considerations, their inclusion acknowledges that some children use these senses to learn or augment learning.

Harcourt Brace School Publishers

Think of children with whom you have worked and see if you can identify a few who rely heavily on one of these modes. Next, think about yourself. Which mode best describes the way *you* learn?

Left brain–Right brain: The Hemisphericity Theory

Another popular theory refers to right- and left-brain functions. Bernice McCarthy, drawing on popular interpretations of brain research, has established a framework for teaching and learning called the 4mat System. The basis of the system is that the left hemisphere of the brain controls such functions as mathematics, sequencing, and systematic and orderly approaches to thinking. The right hemisphere operates in the areas of visual imagery, spatial understanding, and intuition.

McCarthy and others assert that schools have traditionally overemphasized left-brain development at the expense of right-brain functions. For example, curriculum and instruction typically rely on the logical ordering of reading, writing, and math. McCarthy's theory encourages teachers to provide a variety of integrated activities so that children can use *both* halves of their brains.

Howard Gardner's Theory of Multiple Intelligences

For most of this century, human intelligence has been measured by aptitude or IQ tests, in which a child is assigned a single number as a measure of her or his intelligence. These tests typically measure verbal and math abilities that relate directly to what children traditionally do in school. Two major problems have emerged with IQ scores. First, they have been viewed as stable and permanent measures of a child's intelligence. This can limit a child's chances for future learning. Second, this approach to intelligence ignores talents a child might have outside the verbal and mathematical spheres.

Gardner debunks the entire notion of a single measure for intelligence. He has come up with seven clusters that he believes better represent a model of human intelligence. He further asserts that education should systematically provide for all of them, instead of concentrating on the traditional reading, writing, and mathematics curricula. Gardner's seven "intelligences" are

1. **Verbal/Linguistic** The ability to think in words and to use language to acquire, process, and express complex meaning
2. **Musical/Rhythmic** The ability to use melody, rhythm, and pitch to express oneself and to communicate
3. **Logical/Mathematical** The abililty to calculate, quantify, consider propositions and hypotheses, and carry out complex mathematical operations
4. **Visual/Spatial** The ability to think and express oneself in three dimensions, as artists and architects do
5. **Bodily/Kinesthetic** The development of highly refined physical skills, such as dancers, athletes, and artisans have

Harcourt Brace School Publishers

6. Intrapersonal The ability to know oneself clearly and to perceive and develop an accurate and effective internal model for self-direction

7. Interpersonal The capacity to work and communicate effectively with other people, as exhibited by effective teachers, counselors, and politicians

Obviously, many children and adults have strengths in more than one of these intelligences, but some individuals become highly skilled in a single realm. These people should be viewed as highly intelligent, regardless of their performances on traditional IQ tests.

Presenting information effectively

Humans receive most information through their senses of hearing and sight, especially in school. Rich descriptive language can also be used to stimulate sensations of taste, touch, and smell. What you say and how you set up the reading experience for children are critical to their development as learners. In particular, prereading activities that build on children's prior knowledge are essential for enabling children to read for meaning and purpose.

Processing and expressing information effectively

What are children expected to do after they finish reading a selection? It is important that they have opportunities, preferably in all the learning modes, to express their thoughts and feelings. Many of the concerns about learning styles can be addressed if you diversify the ways children respond before, during, and after reading, listening, or viewing. For example, after reading or hearing a story, children should be encouraged to do at least one of the following:

- Act out all or part of the story.
- Draw a picture of the most important event.
- Discuss how the story made them feel.
- Write about the story and share their writing with a small group.
- Describe a personal experience that correlates to the story in some way.
- Construct a graphic organizer to represent the important patterns in the story.

Such activities help children process information in their most natural modes of expression.

Harcourt Brace School Publishers

Support
for Teachers of
Students Acquiring
ENGLISH

by Dr. Eleanor W. Thonis
Wheatland School District in California; former chairperson of
IRA's English as a Second Language Subcommittee
of the Learners with Special Needs Committee

Everyone appears to agree that some modification must be made to accommodate second-language learners. The resources of the school, however, vary greatly from region to region and are not always available to support teachers or children in these efforts. To the extent that the means permit, teachers may benefit from opportunities to attend conferences, workshops, and other professional growth activities.

In the classroom, certain adaptations can make the learning more accessible and relieve the anxieties of children whose home language is different from the language of the school. This article provides practical suggestions for helping second-language children in the classroom. The suggestions fall into one or more of these categories: appreciating the home culture and language, classroom management techniques, and literacy activities.

Appreciating the Home Culture and Language

- Ask children to teach to classmates words of greeting and common phrases from their home language.

- Identify aspects of the children's cultural experiences to use when they write—celebrating national events, welcoming the new year, preparing for birthdays, and so on.

- Invite family members to share their stories, music, art, legends, and folklore. You might also ask them to share their talents in the classroom, demonstrating needlework, origami, and so on.

- Provide literacy activities in the home language with the help of a teacher, parent, or other volunteer who knows both English and the home language.

Classroom Management Techniques

- Provide frequent opportunities for children to communicate in simple English.

- Invite children to work in cooperative groups or in pairs to increase their comfort level and comprehension.

- Be certain that each small group has at least one child who can serve as a mentor or an interpreter.

- Set aside a small part of the classroom where children may go to find material on various reading levels, including some books in the home language.

Literacy Activities

- Use objects, pictures, and posters to encourage small-group or whole-class discussions.

- Arrange centers that are specially equipped for listening, speaking, writing, and reading in the home language and in English.

- Take children on a short walking trip to a store, bank, or post office. Have children help you plan how to get there and what to do; then discuss the trip after returning to class.

- Continue to use predictable books for newcomers to English print.

- Do choral reading, and encourage children to retell parts of the story.

- Use a song that children know, and write some part of it on the board for the children to sing along.

- Suggest that children write stories using whatever language they wish. Encourage them to illustrate the stories.

- Bring in recipes in English for favorite dishes from children's home culture, and prepare simple dishes as a class.

- Collect examples of humor in cartoons or pictures that may be enjoyed in the home language.

- Ask children to suggest a word that is interesting or difficult to say; then have them explore the word's meaning in a variety of contexts. 🍎

Harcourt Brace School Publishers

Second-Language Acquisition

BY **DR. STEPHEN KRASHEN**
Professor of Education
University of Southern California

Just as we process information using the same kind of visual system, we all acquire language in the same way. The process is simple. We acquire language when we understand the language input we receive from other people or from reading.

There is a great deal of evidence for this "input hypothesis." It includes studies that show that methods using more "comprehensible input" (language that children readily understand) are more effective than methods using less, and that those exposed to more comprehensible input outside of school acquire more, and thus understand more, linguistic knowledge. The input hypothesis also claims that we do not acquire language by direct study—by memorizing vocabulary lists, learning rules of grammar, or speaking or writing. Rather, a large vocabulary, grammatical accuracy, and spoken and written fluency are the results of language acquisition—a result of getting comprehensible input—not the causes of language acquisition.

An important corollary of the input hypothesis is the claim that if the child is given enough comprehensible input, all the grammar rules and vocabulary that the child is ready to acquire will be present in the input. In other words, we do not need to worry that certain structures and words are included. If we present language acquirers with enough interesting messages, the language they are ready to acquire will be there.

If the input hypothesis is correct, helping children acquire language must involve, centrally, helping them get comprehensible input. There are two ways of making input more comprehensible: (1) by altering the language we use or (2) by providing context, or background knowledge.

> "There are no set rules of how to talk to a child that can even approach what you unconsciously know. If you concentrate on communicating, everything else will follow."
> – Roger Brown

Pictures

When beginning-language teachers use pictures with language, they are supplying context. Stories are made more comprehensible when teachers show children the pictures in the book.

Physical Movement

That "total physical response" provides context is the reason it works so well (Asher, 1988). In this language-teaching method, teachers give children commands requiring a physical movement—such as "Stand up." In the early stages, the teacher models the actions, which makes the commands more comprehensible.

Language Itself

As children become more proficient, the information provided by language itself can be used as context; unknown individual words and grammatical rules are acquired more readily if they occur in a message that is comprehensible, even in the absence of context provided by the real world.

The First Language

A very powerful means of supplying context is to use the child's first language. Clear support for this idea comes from successful bilingual programs. A good education in children's primary language, and knowledge of subject matter, helps children become more successful in acquiring English because it makes the input they get in English more comprehensible. Similarly, when we read newspapers in other languages, the input is more comprehensible because of the knowledge of the news we obtained through our first language.

Altering the Language We Use

There is no doubt that we often alter our speech to make it easier to understand. We don't talk the same way to a friend as we do to a small child. When speaking to children, our speech is grammatically simpler and sometimes slower and it contains fewer difficult words. Does this mean we should make a conscious effort to change our speech when talking to second-language acquirers? While it is a good idea to talk a bit slower, and to use simpler speech, there are no exact procedures we as teachers should follow in trying to make our speech more comprehensible. We don't have to worry about using fewer relative clauses or making less use of complex tenses. What is crucial is to make sure that what we say is understood. There are many ways to do this, ranging from simply asking, "Did you understand?" (the least precise way) to noting physical reactions (Did the child's behavior indicate comprehension?).

If we monitor comprehension, the input hypothesis tells us, the appropriate structures, and vocabulary will automatically be provided.

Roger Brown gave very similar advice to parents who were interested in accelerating first-language development in their own children:

"Believe that your child can understand more than he or she can say, and seek, above all, to communicate. To understand and be understood. To keep your minds fixed on the same target. In doing that, you will, without thinking about it, make 100 or maybe 1,000 alterations in your speech and action. Do not try to practice them as such. There are no set rules of how to talk to a child that can even approach what you unconsciously know. If you concentrate on communicating, everything else will follow." [Brown (1977), p. 26]

As with spoken input, reading materials need only be comprehensible and interesting to support language acquisition. They need not be "authentic" (written by native speakers

Harcourt Brace School Publishers

for native speakers), and there is nothing inherently wrong with using texts written for second-language acquirers as long as they are interesting and comprehensible.

Supplying Context

Something we can do to make our input more comprehensible is to supply context. Numerous studies have shown that providing context has a dramatic effect on comprehensibility, and common sense confirms this. It is, for example, much easier to understand input in a second language when you have some idea of the subject matter. It is very hard to "eavesdrop" in a second language.

Even when little primary language help is available, it can be very valuable. Consider the case of a class with three Korean-speaking children who know little English. They are progressing fairly well in mathematics because of good math instruction in their first language, and because math does not require a high level of language ability in early grades. Assume that we have a helper who speaks Korean but who is available for one hour only one morning per week. My suggestion is that we inform the helper what is to be studied the following week—in social studies, for example. If it is the Civil War, the helper may use the one hour on Monday to provide the children with background information, in Korean, about the Civil War—who the combatants were, what the issues were, etc. This will make the following week's history lessons much more comprehensible.

While supplying background knowledge in the first language beforehand can be extremely helpful, it is not helpful to supply a running translation. When we do "concurrent translation," the child does not have to attend to the English input, and the teacher does not have to try to make it more comprehensible. This common-sense prediction is confirmed by empirical research. Bilingual programs that rely on concurrent translation do not teach English well. The best way is to use the first language to provide background knowledge, not translation of lessons.

Self-Selected Reading We combine the two ways of making input more comprehensible (supplying simpler input and context) when we encourage children to do self-selected free reading. When children read what they want to read, they select reading material that they find interesting and comprehensible. Better readers have a tendency to read "series" books, books by the same author and/or books on a single topic. Good readers may get hooked on the Sweet Valley or Power Ranger series, for example, or the works of Judy Blume or R. L. Stine. One interpretation of this phenomenon is that such "narrow reading" helps children become good readers. Reading about the same characters or themes provides context and helps make the input more comprehensible, and this increases language and literacy development.

We know that when children are allowed to read what they want to read, they don't simply select easy books. They choose books based on their interests. There is, in addition, evidence that children's choices change and develop as they continue to do self-selected reading, which broadens their knowledge of both languages and the world.

Harcourt Brace School Publishers

What Not to Do

1. Don't correct errors. The research literature clearly shows that correction of children's language is practically useless. Even for older students who understand grammar and who are highly literate, correction results in either no improvement or in very modest improvement that shows up primarily on tests in which students can be focused on form. Accuracy improves when children get more comprehensible input, especially through reading, not when their output is correct.

2. Don't teach grammar. The research literature on grammar teaching is consistent. Grammar teaching has little or no effect on acquisition. Even with older students who understand grammar and who expect and want it, the results are small gains on tests in which students can focus on grammatical correctness, and these gains are typically short-lived. We all want children to speak and write with maximum grammatical accuracy. The way to develop accuracy is not through grammar exercises, however, but through comprehensible input, especially through reading.

3. Don't teach vocabulary. According to research done at the University of Illinois, picking up vocabulary by reading is ten times as efficient, in terms of words learned per minute, as learning through direct vocabulary instruction. Time is therefore better spent in reading. Preteaching vocabulary is also not very efficient. According to research, preteaching concepts provides context and is a big help in making input more comprehensible, but preteaching individual words is much less helpful. Besides if a text or activity requires a great deal of preteaching, it is probably inappropriate.

What to Do: A Summary

1. Provide children with comprehensible input in the classroom. For beginners, use TPR (total physical response), pictures, and other types of context.

2. Don't be overly concerned with making your speech "simple." While it is a good idea to think about "toning down" your speech when speaking to limited-English-proficient children, if you keep your focus on communication, you will automatically change your speech to make it easier to understand.

3. Take advantage of the child's first language to make input more comprehensible. This can be done even if you do not speak that language. The best way is to provide a full bilingual education program. A helper (paraprofessional, older child) may also provide some background knowledge.

4. Encourage free voluntary reading, and allow children to read "narrowly."

It must be more than coincidence that the best way to help children acquire another language is also the easiest and most pleasant way for both teachers and children. Providing comprehensible input via interesting classroom activities and self-selected reading is a more pleasant—and a much more effective—support for language acquisition than grammar drills, error correction, and vocabulary lists. 🍎

Harcourt Brace School Publishers

Fostering HOME LANGUAGE MAINTENANCE

by Dr. Alma Flor Ada

Director of Doctoral Studies
International Multicultural Program
University of San Francisco

Maintaining the ability to speak the language of their families will provide children with academic and professional assets in the future. Fostering a successful interaction with members of their culture strengthens their sense of identity and gives them a firm platform from which to grow.

Unfortunately, most children who grow up in the United States speaking home languages other than English lose the ability to speak their mother tongues to a greater or lesser degree. They very seldom develop full literacy in their home languages.

This process not only leads to the loss of valuable abilities; it also causes children's sense of identity and self-esteem to suffer, and their relationships with their parents as well.

Education can determine the degree to which children maintain or lose their home languages. Maintaining the home language does not require speaking that language. Of course, a good bilingual program is the ideal situation for a child's abilities in the home language to grow and develop. But even within a nonbilingual classroom, a teacher who does not speak the language of the child can facilitate its maintenance and growth.

Children will feel better about their language if they see it related to prestigious activities; thus it is important to have children use the home language by acting as interpreters, translators, researchers, and teachers. Here are some activities that can be carried out at any level.

1. Book Sharing

Encourage children to take home books in the home language and to read them with their families or to have a family member read the books to them.

2. Written Translations

If children are literate in their home language, encourage them to translate children's books from the home language into English. Have them bind and illustrate their books, displaying the child's name as translator on the cover.

3. Development of Interpreting Skills

Show appreciation for children's translating or interpreting skills. Ask children to serve as interpreters for visitors, community members, or elders. Invite bilingual children to interview or translate interviews with monolingual children in the class.

4. Children as Researchers

Encourage children to discuss with their parents what they are learning in school, using the home language. Have children share their parents' feedback with the class.

5. Children as Storytellers

Have children ask their families to write or share their family's history and illustrate it with photos and artifacts. Children can then share the history with the class.

6. Children as Teachers

Encourage children to teach everyone in the class a few phrases or sentences in their home language. Have everyone learn to say *hello, good-bye, thank you,* and *please* in every language represented in the class. Incorporate these expressions into everyday classroom conversations, and add new ones as appropriate.

7. International Chorus

Have children learn a song or poem in their home language and teach it to the class.

8. Building Bridges

Provide editions in children's home languages of the literature books you are studying or reading with the whole class. Let children read, or at least find in the book, some words they recognize in their home language. (In some languages they may be able to find word cognates with similar spellings in two languages, for example, *kilo*.) Have children take the books home and share them with their families.

Harcourt Brace School Publishers

EARLY INTERVENTION:
KEY COMPONENT OF A SUCCESSFUL READING PROGRAM

by Dr. Dorothy S. Strickland
State of New Jersey Professor of Reading, Rutgers University

During the past few decades, educators have placed increasing amounts of energy and funding into remedial programs designed to help children who are experiencing difficulty in learning to read and write. It is not uncommon for a student to spend several years in such programs during the elementary grades, only to enter middle school still far behind grade-level expectations. The research is clear that remediation is not doing the job. In recent years a growing and very impressive body of research has been amassed to suggest that early intervention may be a much more promising answer to this perennial problem.

Research findings show that intervention is less costly than years of remediation, less costly than retention, and—ultimately—less costly to children's self-esteem. This final point may be the most compelling, since the savings in human suffering and humiliation is incalculable. Teachers in remedial programs observe that children who feel they are failures frequently give up and stop trying to learn, despite good instruction. Here is what the research, based on several successful early intervention programs, says about the components of an effective early intervention program.

Research findings show that intervention is less costly than years of remediation, less costly than retention, and— ultimately—less costly to children's self-esteem.

WHAT MAKES A GOOD EARLY INTERVENTION PROGRAM?

TIME AND TIMING

- **More time on task is not enough. It's also what you do during that time that counts.**

- **Programs usually span part or all of the first grade. Some begin in kindergarten. Some children require continued help in second grade.**

Using Little Books designed for emergent readers, such as the Harcourt Brace *Instant Readers,* provides a strong early intervention thrust at grade one. Continued support is made available for those children who may need further help and those who may be new to the program at later levels.

MATERIALS

- **Use texts that children can read successfully.**

- **Gradually increase difficulty.**

Little Books such as the *Instant Readers* are leveled for reading difficulty so that teachers can make an appropriate fit of child to book. Struggling readers experience immediate success, giving them the confidence to take the necessary risks involved in gradually mastering harder and harder material.

INSTRUCTION

- **Work to ensure quality instruction in both regular and intervention programs.**

Intervention strategies provide support to those children who need a second or third try at certain early reading strategies already introduced to the entire class.

Additional instruction should be consistent with the skill development offered in the core reading program, while making use of fresh and entertaining material.

- **Tailor intervention strategies to individual and small-group needs.**

Teachers should observe any problems during whole-group activities and make use of flexible grouping in order to provide small-group and individual instruction for those who need additional help.

- **Spend less time on isolated skills and traditional workbook practice, more time on meaningful reading and writing.**

Spending more time on reading and responding to whole texts is fundamental. Skills and strategies are taught within the context of meaningful literature. Skills are not taught simply to be accumulated; they are taught to be used.

- **Combine reading and writing as meaning construction with systematic word identification strategies, using all three cueing systems (phonics, word meaning, sentence structure).**

Phonics must be given strong, systematic treatment. In order to make it optimally effective, it should be combined with word meaning and sentence structure, which are equally important word identification skills.

- **Provide many opportunities for writing.**

Use suggestions for group and independent writing to help children respond to literature, express personal ideas, and apply what they have learned about phonics and the conventions of written language.

Harcourt Brace School Publishers

- **Involve children in repeated readings of texts.**

Repeated reading of the same material gives children a sense of confidence and helps develop fluency. Opportunities for repeated reading include choral reading, partner reading, reading selected parts, and reading aloud at home.

ASSESSMENT

- **Plan for systematic assessment to monitor progress and to develop instructional planning. Use informal daily monitoring of fluency, word recognition, and comprehension.**

Various techniques for monitoring children's progress, including the use of running records, checklists, and systematic observations, are suggested and explained in the Assessment section of this Staff Development Guide, pages 117-134.

HOME/SCHOOL CONNECTION

- **Include reading at home and opportunities for parent participation.**

Instant Readers® and other Little Books are perfect for sharing—with family members at home—a child's success in learning to read. Children and parents take pride in observing a child's proficiency in reading increasingly difficult books.

SUMMARY

In summary, much has been learned about how to prevent failure in reading and writing. Quality early intervention is critical for many children, but it cannot stand alone. It works best in conjunction with a strong core program. Materials must be easy enough to allow children to feel a sense of achievement and then gradually increase in difficulty.

Early intervention is more focused than regular instruction. It should be customized to the learner's specific needs as determined by systematic observation and monitoring of progress.

Integrate instruction in reading and writing so that what children learn about one serves to enhance their learning of the other. Word identification should also be taught in an integrated way. Children need to learn how to use phonics, word meaning, and sentence structure in a combined way in order to help them make sense of what they read and what they write for others to read.

Finally, early intervention programs must connect to the home. Parents need to be aware of the efforts being made on behalf of their children, and they need to participate in the process.

Harcourt Brace School Publishers

Reading Success for Low-Achieving Children

by Edna Cucksey-Stephens • Language Arts Consultant, Clarkston, Michigan

Low-achieving children present us with some of our most challenging teaching. They can also provide some of our most rewarding experiences. The belief that all children can become successful readers is the key to our teaching and their learning. Low achievers often need more of our time and patience, but they benefit from the same meaning-based, holistic instruction as other children.

These reluctant readers often see themselves as "not very good" at reading. They may have poor self-esteem and sometimes feel "stupid" when their reading is not successful. The following ideas and suggestions will empower these children to be more self-confident about their reading ability and thus improve their reading success.

Conference individually with low-achieving children.

- Communicate your belief that they can succeed.
- Explain that you will be a partner in their learning.
- Discuss reading as an interactive process in which the reader is just as important as the text.
- Stress meaning and "making sense."
- Accept children's personal responses to texts.
- Talk about children's interests and the types of books that build on those interests.
- Ask what they think you and they can do to help them become better readers.

- Stress that children who are not yet good readers are not "stupid." They just need to learn good reading strategies.
- Discuss the idea that using strategies can make reading easier and more fun.

Teach and model good reading strategies.

Many children do not discover reading strategies on their own. Teachers must teach strategies directly. Talk about what a strategy is and why it is important. Point out the following:

- Good readers set purposes for reading.
- Good readers look at titles, pictures, and graphics to help them figure out words.
- Good readers always try to make sense of what they read.

Stress that readers of all ability levels can learn and use these strategies. Explain and model **what** these strategies are, **how** they should be used, **why** they are important, and **when** they should be used.

Ask often: "What strategy should you use when you come to a word you do not know?" Encourage children to read an unfamiliar word as a blank, to finish the sentence, and then to come back to see what word would make sense. Also, connect these strategies to content-area reading in other parts of the curriculum.

Harcourt Brace School Publishers

Explain the reading program and good reading strategies to family members.

- This can be done at a meeting or through a newsletter and will enable families to better help their children at home.
- Help parents and guardians understand that they play a crucial part in their children's learning and reading success.
- Stress the importance of encouraging children to read at home every day.

Provide varied types of instruction.

- Whole-group instruction allows children to interact with other children and benefit from discussion.
- Small-group instruction enables the teacher to monitor reading progress and provide skills instruction in meaningful context.

- Individual instruction allows teachers to focus on individual needs and accomplishments.
- Listening centers are particularly helpful to auditory learners and to students acquiring English as a second language.

Encourage prediction.

- Prediction sets purposes for reading.
- Encourage children to read to confirm their predictions, but stress that predictions cannot turn out "wrong." Children should feel free to change their predictions as they read.
- Prediction helps keep children on task. Children tend to stay focused when they are reading to find out what will happen next.

Encourage risk-taking.

- Help children understand that making errors is a natural part of learning.
- Don't accept "I don't know" and "I can't." Respond with invitations such as "What do you think?" or "What's your best guess?"
- Give positive reinforcement whenever possible.
- Allow adequate "wait time" for children to answer questions. If they're stumped, rephrase your question.

Engage in activities that produce confidence. Here are some examples:

- Read the text to children before expecting them to read it on their own.
- Use language experience stories based on children's interests. (See also "Strategies for Reluctant Learners," pages 111–114.)
- Use group activities such as shared reading, echo reading, choral reading, partner reading, and Readers Theatre. Repeated readings build confidence and help children focus on meaning. Use think-alouds during oral readings to model good reading strategies.
- Reread for expression and fluency.
- Reread children's favorite part of the story.

Build on what is known.

- Encourage children to look at a familiar word to figure out an unfamiliar word. For example, if the unfamiliar word is *small,* write the word *all,* and say, "You know this word." Have a child say the word. "Since this word is *all,* then this word must be _____."
- Connect learning to children's background experiences and interests.

Teach vocabulary and skills in meaningful contexts.

- Teaching vocabulary and skills in meaningful context helps children make sense and purpose of the learning.
- Whenever possible, show an unfamiliar word in several different contexts.
- Teach skills such as sequence, main idea, and cause and effect as they relate to stories students have read *and* to "real-life" situations.

Look for activities that older children can do with younger children.

- Children can share with younger children by reading to them, developing a puppet show about a story, writing stories together, and even modeling or teaching a lesson.

Help children see evidence of their progress.

- Tape-record children as they read orally.
- Replay the tape in a month or so. Talk about the progress that has been made and what children notice about their reading. This is an excellent way for children, teachers, and children's families to monitor reading progress.
- Use the tape to determine the strategies the child is using and strategies that need to be further developed.

Read aloud to children every day.

- Reading aloud models fluency.
- Reading aloud is an opportunity to model what good readers do.
- As children follow along in their copies of a story, words that they recognize orally become words they can recognize in print.
- You may wish to tape-record some of the stories you read. These tapes can be used by children in a listening center.

Harcourt Brace School Publishers

STRATEGIES *for* RELUCTANT LEARNERS:

A CONVERSATION WITH
DR. BARBARA BOWEN COULTER

—

Dr. Barbara Bowen Coulter is Director of Communication Arts in the Detroit Public Schools.

Q Who are the reluctant learners in primary-level classrooms?

A Usually, they are the children who have had few experiences with print, stories, and books. We need to think of them as "inexperienced." Print-rich, story-rich, book-rich classrooms are important for all learners; however, they are critical for children who have had limited experiences in literacy activities.

Jim Trelease has reminded us that there are five times as many video stores as there are public libraries and that most American adults don't read even one book a year. It should come as no surprise to us, then, that some children come to school having had little or no experience with books.

Q What does the research say about reluctant learners?

A Almost all children can learn to read and write, and they really want to. The first three years of school are critical. A teacher must find out what the children know and then do whatever is appropriate to help them expand their capabilities.

Learned helplessness and patterns of negative thinking can lead to a lack of personal responsibility for learning. Unfortunately, children who experience frustration and failure in literacy activities begin to believe that they can't do it; they appear to lack confidence.

Q We use reading anthologies and trade books in my classroom. What other resources should I provide for reluctant learners?

A The patterned language and predictable structure of poetry, finger plays, nursery rhymes, and songs allow learners to participate almost immediately in a literacy event. With each rereading of a text, they might be tracking print, reading chorally, reading with partners, echo reading, or just singing a favorite song for the sheer joy of it.

Q I have so much to get through in my current reading program, yet some of my students are not keeping up. Is there really time for me to add even more materials?

A Children learn by doing, by having fun, and by feeling important. Poetry and songs can be used to enrich instruction and to give *all* kids a chance to feel good about themselves in school. Poetry and songs also immerse reluctant learners in the dominant language at school so that language patterns are heard, read, sung, and dramatized over and over again.

Listen, for example, to the patterns in the familiar round "Are You Sleeping?"

Are you sleep-ing, are you sleep-ing,
Bro-ther John? Bro-ther John?
Morn-ing bells are ring-ing, Morn-ing bells are ring-ing.
Ding, Ding, Dong! Ding, Ding, Dong!

Q Even my most hard-to-reach students really enjoy the storytelling time in our school library. Why is this?

A Storytelling is part of every culture worldwide, and it's been with us forever. Why not make the best use of its inherent appeal? Perhaps you could develop a storyteller theme or unit. Children can learn the art of storytelling in the same manner that the ancient storyteller or griot acquired the skill; that is, by observing and listening to storytellers. The students will see teachers as their role models; they will see that their teachers value stories.

Q Fine, but I don't feel comfortable right now with my storytelling ability. How can I become better at it?

A Family stories are the best place to start because you know them so well; perhaps you're even the main character! Family folklore is the creative expression of a common past; it can include props, costumes, and photographs.

GUIDELINES FOR STORYTELLING
- Choose a story with great child appeal that you know very well.
- Memorization is not necessary. Rehearse the story a few times to get a feeling for the sequence and major events. Story mapping may be done, too.
- Plan interesting phrases or repeated phrases to enliven the language of your story.
- Use simple props or gestures to increase the group's interest.
- Prepare a brief introduction.
- Practice telling your story in front of a mirror.

Harcourt Brace School Publishers

"FAMILY FOLKLORE IS THE CREATIVE EXPRESSION OF A COMMON PAST."

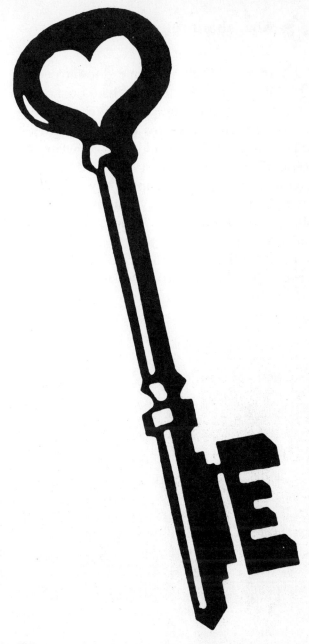

Q Describe how you would have children participate in a storytelling theme.

A Have them follow the same steps you do in becoming a storyteller. First, be sure they're exposed to several storytellers, preferably with a variety of styles. Then assign as homework an interview with family members, and have children select one family story to perform. Be sensitive, however, to any child's reluctance to do this, for whatever reason. If some children prefer to retell a folktale or a favorite piece of contemporary literature or sing a song, by all means honor and respect their decision.

What about reluctant writers?

 How would a storytelling theme benefit reluctant learners?

Your storytelling theme doesn't end after every student has had a chance to be a storyteller for the group. Writing activities can precede and flow from each storyteller's performance. Children may write in response journals, develop a calendar of events, or make story maps. They could also create advertisements, invitations, and even playbills for their "show." These are all valid and exciting writing experiences that even reluctant writers will enjoy. To help them get started, let children work collaboratively if they wish.

Storytelling provides equity for reluctant learners; that is, the feelings of failure and frustration they cope with in other activities are offset by the successes they enjoy during storytelling. Success is assured because each individual chooses selections in which he or she is interested and then develops the presentation according to his or her interests and abilities. Thus, children are practicing and applying language arts strategies within a context that is very meaningful to them.

Harcourt Brace School Publishers

THE GIFTED CHILD

by Dr. W. Dorsey Hammond

Although the experts don't agree on a single definition of giftedness, there is a body of research describing the classroom practices that best stimulate, challenge, and nurture the special strengths of gifted and talented children. In planning curriculum for these children, keep these points in mind:

- Children may be gifted in one area but not in another.
- Gifted children are not always the highest achievers.
- Gifted children are not always the most socially mature.
- *Creative* children may or may not be the most *intellectually* advanced.
- Giftedness shows up at different levels of development. With some children, the giftedness is obvious; with others, we see the potential, but it needs nurturing to emerge.
- Giftedness seldom develops to full potential without teaching, coaching, encouragement, mentoring, and modeling.

For the child gifted with an extraordinary memory . . .

Provide comfortable, inviting settings for children to share what they have learned about a topic that interests them. Encourage them to use graphic organizers such as K-W-L charts and prediction charts as part of their presentation to a group. Since these children's interests may be quite sophisticated, you may need to coach them to keep their audience in mind as they plan what they will say and show, how they will explain it, and how they will keep their listeners interested.

For the child gifted with a highly developed imagination . . .

All children eventually become bored with routine tasks, but gifted and talented children may reach a level of competency much sooner than their peers. When they're ready for something else to do, put them to work helping you! Some children might enjoy transforming a set of learning tasks into a game format; for example, making

games for specific phonics skills. Encourage children to work with a partner to create game boards, game pieces, and rules for a game that will appeal to their classmates. Other children might prefer to research a topic in depth and plan a presentation—diorama, play, book—that makes good use of their talents.

For the child gifted with unusual musical, artistic, or athletic ability . . .

Ask these children to help you plan and carry out a special literacy event based on their area of expertise. For example, a Literary Field Day might feature activity stations set up outdoors or in a gym. Each activity station represents one book the children know well. Small groups of children travel from station to station, completing a literature-based activity and receiving a badge for their efforts. By the end of the field day, everyone's a winner!

For the child gifted with unusual writing or dramatic ability . . .

These children can help you establish and maintain two of your most important learning centers: the writing/publishing center and the dramatic play center. Ask children to work collaboratively on furnishing the centers with different props, depending on the stories the class is reading. These children can write and direct original plays, compile big books and poetry collections, present puppet shows, and write and illustrate books for younger children. These children can also be encouraged to help other children make comparisons and connections among books, themes, authors, illustrators, and so on.

For the child gifted with unusual mathematical ability . . .

Don't forget the computer! Of course, children with all kinds of special talents can benefit from time on the computer, providing the software meets their needs and ability levels. But certain programs are particularly well suited to children whose ways of thinking about math concepts, patterns, and relationships are especially unique.

Every child presents us with new challenges and opportunities. Gifted and talented children enrich our entire classroom and make learning more exciting for everyone. Look for giftedness in every child; then do what you can to nurture and promote it!

Harcourt Brace School Publishers

Assessment

" *...**P**ut the emphasis in assessment squarely where it belongs: on what children know and can do.*"

Dr. Roger Farr

Kid WATCHING

Primary teachers are continually monitoring children's development. They start by establishing the emotional as well as the physical environment for learning. Within this context, they offer children many kinds of experiences. Some involve teacher-guided group instruction, such as shared reading and response to literature. Other experiences, such as center-based activities, are geared more to cooperative learning and personal choice. Still other activities involve teacher and child in one-on-one instruction.

Effective teachers know that by "kid watching" as children participate in these activities, they can build a viable profile of each child as a learner. Kid watching, the process of monitoring children's ongoing development through daily activities that are integral to instruction, is at the center of such an assessment program.

Putting the kid-watching philosophy to work in the primary classroom involves *observation, interaction,* and *analysis* (Y. M. Goodman, 1989, p. 8).

Observation includes the examination of what children are doing as the teacher stands on the sidelines. Very often, the teacher focuses on an individual child working independently or as a member of a group. (See the checklists on pages 128–134 of this guide.)

Sometimes, however, the teacher may also want to watch a small group of children in action during independent reading or center time. Are they making use of print in the environment? Do they seem to be applying strategies introduced during teacher-guided instruction? Are the materials in the center serving their purpose? How might the center function more effectively?

by Dr. Roger Farr

Dr. Roger Farr is Chancellors' Professor of Education and Director of the Center for Reading and Language Studies, Indiana University.

One way to streamline your note taking when observing is to jot down impressions on gummed labels. Later, put them in a child's folder or portfolio or in your own records about center activity.

Interaction enables a teacher to gather information during conferences about work in progress. A teacher's questions help both teacher and child discover what the child knows. (See pages 120–121.) Teacher-child dialogues about a story or a drawing, the "reading" of a favorite book, or the literacy events that occur during free-play activities yield excellent information about how well a child is using his or her emergent literacy.

Most often, these interactions will be brief encounters that take advantage of opportune or "teachable" moments. For that reason, it helps to keep note cards or other materials handy at all times for record keeping.

Analysis of children's literacy activities—reading stories, writing responses to a story, inventing conversations between two home-made puppets—requires an in-depth study of children's language awareness and language use. A teacher uses his or her psycholinguistic and sociolinguistic knowledge to understand where children are and what can be done to help them progress as readers and writers.

Information from these three processes helps confirm what a teacher may already know intuitively about his or her children. Page 25 describes how these kid-watching tools may be used during a shared reading.

PORTFOLIO CONFERENCES

BY DR. ROGER FARR

Portfolio conferences are really quite simple. All you have to do is remember that a conference is a time for sharing and that you are having a conversation with a person who has much to offer. The following guidelines outline some of the essentials:

- **Let the child do most of the talking.** You will learn much more about the child if you let him or her talk.

- **Avoid being evaluative.** Respect the child as a learner. If you think of the conference as a time for the child to reflect on his or her own reading and writing, you will be less judgmental.

- **Avoid interruptions.** Children need our undivided attention during a conference. If you are constantly interrupted, the child will be unable to develop his or her ideas. Also, if you allow constant interruptions, the child may conclude that this one-to-one discussion is not very important to you.

- **Ask questions that open up conversations rather than shut down communication.** Use open-ended questions that ask for explanations, expansions, examples, and discussion. You learn more about children when they explain, justify, clarify, and express their ideas and beliefs. The quality of the responses will depend on the quality of the questions you ask. Children will provide more explanations if they believe that you are interested in and truly respect them and their opinions.

- **Use the conference as a time to plan goals with the child.** Ask questions such as the following: What do you plan to read or write about next? What are you planning to do with this story? How can I help you?

- **Write notes about what you have learned.** Take time after each conference to jot down notes about the conference and the goals you and the child have discussed. Add the notes to the child's portfolio so they can be reviewed at the next conference.

Harcourt Brace School Publishers

CONFERENCE CHECKLIST

Reading and Writing Focus

☐ gives the most important purpose for reading and writing

☐ is willing to share ideas

☐ shows confidence and takes risks in experimenting with new ideas

☐ uses information from other models, from other authors and genres, or from friends

☐ explores personal interests through reading and writing

☐ is aware of audience

Reading and Writing Strategies and Conventions

☐ indicates sources of ideas, such as personal experiences or reading

☐ gives evidence of how feedback from others has been incorporated into reading and writing

☐ uses expressive language to discuss a previously read book or a selected piece of writing

☐ connects ideas logically in organizational schemes such as comparison and contrast, cause and effect, or time sequence

GENERAL QUESTION/STATEMENT	FOLLOW-UP QUESTIONS
1. **Tell me how you use your portfolio.**	Why did you organize your portfolio this way? How did you decide which pieces to include in your portfolio?
2. **Tell me about one story in your portfolio.**	Why is this story important to you? Why did you choose to write this? Where did you get the idea? Would you like to read it to me? Did you have any problem writing it?
3. **Tell me about a book that you have read.**	Explain to me why this book is important to you. Why did you decide to read this book? Why would someone else like reading it?
4. **What are you going to read and write next?**	How can I help you with this? What will you do first? Is there someone with whom you would like to work?

Harcourt Brace School Publishers

NAME _____

	YES	SOMETIMES	NO

1. I look at the cover and think of what the story will be about.　☐　☐　☐

2. I use the pictures to help me understand the story.　☐　☐　☐

3. I can see in my mind what I am reading about.　☐　☐　☐

4. I think about what may happen next in the story.　☐　☐　☐

5. I go back and read things again when they don't make sense.　☐　☐　☐

6. When I come to a word I don't know, I _____

_____.

7. When I get to the end of a story, I sometimes _____

_____.

On the back is a picture from my favorite story.

Harcourt Brace School Publishers

NAME _____

	YES	SOMETIMES	NO

1. I think about what I want to write. ☐ ☐ ☐

2. I can see in my mind what I am writing about. ☐ ☐ ☐

3. When I write, I think about who will read my writing. ☐ ☐ ☐

4. I read over my writing to make it better. ☐ ☐ ☐

5. I share my work with a classmate. ☐ ☐ ☐

6. I will draw a line around the things that I like to write.

   story   poem   report   note

7. Something I do well as a writer is _____

   _____

ASSESSING THE DEVELOPMENT OF EMERGENT WRITERS

BY DR. ROGER FARR

Assessment of emergent writing is, quite simply, the thoughtful and appreciative observation of how children express themselves with pictures and symbols. Because what the child wants to say is not always immediately apparent from the marks he or she has put on the paper, this assessment also requires the evaluator to *listen* to the child's ideas about his or her writing. These conversations should encourage the child to become a self-assessor.

"Assessment is directly linked to instruction and is in itself instructional."

Harcourt Brace School Publishers

What are the typical forms of emergent writing?

 Picture drawing as a kind of language Anyone who has talked with very young children about their drawings knows that these pictures have meaning just as surely as a written or oral story has meaning. The child can tell the story that is represented by the pictures. The pictures often present ideas and rich details that go beyond the verbal story.

Scribble writing As children experience more and more literacy events, they begin to understand that the black marks on a page next to a picture carry meaning. And so they begin to mimic those symbols by pretend or scribble writing. To the child, however, this scribbling is just as surely writing as is the print on a page. Often these "scribbles" include both odd-shaped letters and pictures woven together. The scribble writing may extend horizontally, from left to right, and with some erratic sense of margins and placement on a page.

Letter strings At some point, young writers begin stringing together letters and shapes that approximate letters, frequently within a line of scribbling. These letters have been observed by the child in signs and books and on TV; often, too, children have had exposure to them in school activities. Some children will tie drawings into this very early writing in fascinating attempts to communicate.

Invented spelling Children surrounded by print and familiar with the alphabet will eventually begin to tie letter sounds to individual letters in order to communicate more effectively. Given ample opportunity to read and write, alone and within a group, children feel free to take risks in how they spell words.

 How can I read scribble writing?

 Have the child read it to you! Observational research has demonstrated that many children can retell their stories—following their scribbling—in much the same way they tell them *as* they scribble. This suggests that for them the scribbling has more literal representation than may be presumed. Don't be concerned that the story is longer or shorter than the scribble writing seems to indicate. Also, don't be concerned that the story changes each time the child tells it. The important point is that you and the child get a sense that the marks on the page can and do represent a story.

 When does conventional spelling begin?

 It actually begins with the use of letter strings. These are conventional spellings, often in fairly consistent patterns. However, they are not the spelling forms that are acceptable to the public. Those acceptable spellings will come naturally as children read and write more. For the vast majority of children, you'll see a definite progression toward more and more conventional spelling, idea structures, and punctuation, particularly when children enjoy daily, intense exposure to print. The content, too, becomes more semantically and syntactically acceptable. The teacher can watch for other signs of progress as well. For example, the child begins to use words that relate ideas temporally, spatially, and in other ways. The complexity of the stories told and ideas expressed, the emergence of a distinctive writer's "voice," and attempts at conventions such as dialogue develop along with more mechanical concerns such as spelling and capitalization.

 Some of my children seem to use several forms of writing within the same piece. Should I be concerned about this?

 Researchers have documented developmental sequences in which drawing and different types of writing/printing may appear. However, these sequences can vary according to the individual child and that child's experience with language. Conventional writing doesn't develop in a rigid hierarchical sequence; children may move back and forth among several writing forms as they experiment with what they already know and what they have just learned. Also, the amount of time that a child wants to devote to a particular piece will influence the forms he or she uses.

Q **What about assessing content, specifically, a child's ability to string together story events and his or her choice of words?**

A Evaluators certainly want to know about an emergent writer's sense of *story*: elements such as logical ordering of events, character development, and cause and effect. Children will vary tremendously in their ability to include a beginning, a middle, and an ending; again, these concepts don't develop in a predictable, linear fashion. It is best to listen to what the child says about his or her story; the complexity of his or her ideas will probably surprise you!

Whether a child has a sense of story can be determined with oral retellings of favorite stories that have been read to or with the child. (See the assessment checklist on page 128.) Listen for similarities to the stories you have been reading to the children. Some children will be more proficient users of story elements and will use a much richer vocabulary to retell story events. However, as you read and discuss more and more stories, you will find that *all* of your children are developing a greater knowledge of story elements.

Being the singular individuals that they are, children devise unique ways to convey information that is important to them. Given the freedom and encouragement to do so, the child will develop a kind of individualistic writing style as his or her own *voice*.

Q **Some of my children seem unsure of their own writing and insist on dictating their stories to me. How can I assess these?**

A You have a wonderful opportunity to find out about the child's reading and to emphasize with the child that writing is talk written down. Write the story for the child and then have him or her read it back to you. You will learn a great deal about story knowledge and reading development this way. (By the way, help the child with any words he or she does not know.) If you continue this type of activity, it won't be long before the reluctant writer is beginning to pen his or her own stories. This is an excellent example of how good assessment and good instruction tie together naturally.

Q **I really hesitate to judge young children's efforts, especially children who are just beginning to take risks in their writing. Should I be correcting all of the "errors" I see in their writing? Should I attempt to put a grade on their papers?**

A The answer to both questions is an unequivocal NO! You're absolutely right to be concerned about the message you're sending emerging writers when you "grade" their work. Instead, think of your role as being an encouraging guide. Basically, your task is to be watching (really, with young children, you're doing more *listening*) for *the student's developing awareness of himself or herself as a writer communicating with particular audiences!* For this to occur, the child must be given ample opportunity to talk about the things he or she is writing and the teacher must observe over *a period of time*. A teacher who regards assessment as a kind of encouraging, benign guidance is doing the very best for children.

We have learned from research and classroom practice that when emerging writers are concerned about making mistakes, their growth in writing stops! Suddenly, they're constantly asking how to spell a word, whether this is the right way to say something, and where to put capital letters and periods. Concern with telling a story and taking risks with language is lost, and growth in writing is surely stunted.

Harcourt Brace School Publishers

How is all of this assessment used?

Perhaps the most dangerous concept about assessment is that it is done separately from instruction. Good assessment is *part* of instruction. The observations you make, the notes you take, and the discussions you have with students are the "stuff" of assessment. What you learn about your group of emerging writers should immediately impact the kinds of literacy experiences you provide in your classroom. For example, suppose you feel that several children show a weak sense of story. You would then make a special effort to include discussions of the beginning, middle, and ending of stories they are reading. Or, if your children exhibit a limited awareness of the audience for whom they write, you might expand their opportu-nities for sharing with other age groups. This is the best way for them to experience first-hand the importance of keeping the audience in mind during the writing process.

* * * *

All children have an important story to tell and a voice as individualistic as any adult's. This deserves our utmost respect. By focusing primarily on children's ideas, but also watching for and guiding the increasing use of language conventions, we put the emphasis in assessment squarely where it belongs: on what children know and *can* do. More importantly, our efforts should always emphasize helping children understand their writing development. As they begin to self-assess their writing, they are developing into writers who always consider the needs and purposes of their audiences.

Basic Guidelines

1. Assessment is directly linked to instruction and is in itself instructional.

2. Always assess what the child *can* do. Give every child a chance to be successful.

3. Listen to the language children use to talk about their writing. This by itself reveals a great deal about their development as writers.

4. Help children become self-assessors. Look for a growing understanding of the functions of reading and writing.

5. Try not to think of reading and writing as separate assessments. A child's literacy development includes both reading and writing, as well as oral language. Don't compartmentalize your assessment. Make sure the assessment of writing helps you and the child to make connections between all of the language arts.

6. Look for growth *over time* in a writer's awareness of

   - audience and purpose.

   - story elements—character; setting; story problem; beginning, middle, ending; dialogue; etc.

   - print conventions—word spacing, letterforms, punctuation, capital letters, etc.

7. Encourage children to take risks. This is how they come to use more conventional forms of writing.

DIRECTIONS Place in front of the child three books that are familiar to him or her. Choose books with a story line rather than ABC or other basic concept books. Ask the child to select one of the books. Explain that he or she is to start at the beginning and read it to you as well as he or she can. Using the chart below, enter today's date next to the state of emergent reading that best describes the child's rendering of the story. The same chart may be reused for each assessment.

Name _____   Teacher _____

	Date	Date	Date
Picture-governed, story not formed (Child reads by labeling and commenting on pictures. Little or no evidence of connected story line.)			
Picture-governed, oral language used (Child focuses on pictures and uses an oral language style in narration. May tell an interesting story, but language is unlike that of book.)			
Picture-governed, more written language used (Child alternates between oral language style and "reading intonation" and wording that sounds like written language. At times, rendering might sound very much like written language of book.)			
Print-governed (Child reads text in conventional manner.)			

CHILD'S NAME _____

TEACHER'S NAME _____

GRADE _____ **SCHOOL** _____

DATE OF READING CONFERENCE _____

Name someone who is a good reader. Why do you think so?

_____

What do you do before you begin to read?

_____

What do you do when you see a word you don't know?

_____

What do you do when something doesn't make sense to you when you are reading?

_____

What do you do when you need help while you are reading?

_____

What is the hardest thing about learning to read?

_____

What would you do if you were going to help someone learn to read?

_____

Book title _____

Strengths we discussed _____

Progress we discussed _____

Problems we discussed _____

Child concerns _____

Teacher suggestions _____

Running Records

by Dr. Roger C. Farr,
Chancellors' Professor of Education and
Director of the Center for Reading and Language Studies, Indiana University

Running Records

A running record can be used to learn about a child's reading strategies.[1] The best approach is to have the child choose a selection that he or she would *like* to read. While the child reads aloud, you record everything that he or she says or does. Use the form on page 131 to help you record the reading.

Running records are usually based on a child's reading of 100 to 200 words. On a copy of the selection, mark the miscues as directed on the chart below. After the child has finished reading, check comprehension by asking the child to tell you about the selection.

After the running-record activity is completed, you will be able to review it and note the child's reading strategies and miscue patterns. This information can be very valuable in planning reading instruction and determining how the child is developing as a strategic reader.

[1] The concept of a running record was developed by Marie Clay and is explained more fully in her book *An Observation: Survey of Early Literacy Achievement,* Portsmouth, NH: Heinemann, 1993.

Marking Oral Reading Miscues		
Reading Miscue	**Marking**	**Sample**
1. omissions	Circle the word, word part, or phrase omitted.	I will let you ⊙go in.
2. insertions	Insert a caret (∧), and write in the inserted word or phrase.	We bought a∧parrot. *(big)*
3. substitutions	Write the word or phrase the student substitutes over the word or phrase in the text.	Dad fixed ~~my~~ bike. *(the)*
4. mispronunciations	Write the phonetic mispronunciation over the word.	Have you ~~fed~~ the dog? *(feed)*
5. self-corrections	Write the letters *SC* next to the miscue that is self-corrected.	We took our ~~space~~ sc. *(spots)*
6. repetitions	Draw a line under any part of the text that is repeated.	It is your <u>garden</u> now.
7. punctuation	Circle punctuation missed. Write in any punctuation inserted.	Take them home⊙Then come back,and you and I will go to town.
8. hesitations	Place vertical lines at places where the student hesitates excessively.	Pretend|this is mine.

Harcourt Brace School Publishers

Oral Reading Checklist

CHILD'S NAME ______________________________

TEACHER'S NAME ______________________________

GRADE __________ **SCHOOL** ______________________________

MARKING KEY	
+	Consistently
○	Occasionally
−	Never

DATE						
Tracks print successfully						
Uses punctuation marks effectively						
Applies basic phonetic generalizations and exceptions						
Skips difficult words or phrases to stay focused on meaning						
Rereads if things don't make sense						
Self-corrects errors						
Adds to the text only words that make sense contextually						
Demonstrates a sense of story						

CHILD'S NAME _____

TEACHER'S NAME _____

MARKING KEY	
+	Consistently
○	Occasionally
−	Never

DATE

Uses print as well as pictures to convey meaning					
Writes from left to right					
Leaves a space between words or groups of letters meant to represent words					
Sounds out letters while writing words (i.e., shows an awareness that letters represent sounds and that words can be segmented into phonemes)					
Displays an awareness of grammar when writing sentences					
Displays an awareness of punctuation					
Evaluates his or her writing or drawing and the writing or drawing of peers					

COMMENTS _____

_____

Harcourt Brace School Publishers

CHILD'S NAME _____

TEACHER'S NAME _____

MARKING KEY	
+	Consistently
○	Occasionally
−	Never

DATE						
Speaking						
Volunteers for speaking activities						
Makes comments that are appropriate to the situation						
Expresses ideas clearly and accurately						
Uses information accurately						
Supports point of view with logical evidence						
Responds logically to comments of others						
Rephrases or adjusts if others don't understand						
Takes turns in group discussions						
Listening						
Attends to what others are saying						
Exhibits reactions (e.g., facial expressions) that reflect comprehension						
Understands directions without needing repetition						
Ignores distractions						

COMMENTS _____

Harcourt Brace School Publishers

Despite changes in instructional practices and new ways of assessing and evaluating children's progress, most teachers are still faced with the task of giving grades. Using a rubric such as the one shown below for rating a child's comprehension of a story, you can get a letter or numerical score on a holistic task. As long as you identify the criteria *before* you score children's work, the grading is not subjective at all.

Story Comprehension

CHILD _____ **DATE** _____

Child understands the story.	4	3	2	1
Child understands how main character feels.	4	3	2	1
Child recalls significant details.	4	3	2	1
Child notes cause-and-effect relationships.	4	3	2	1
Child generates questions and makes thoughtful comments.	4	3	2	1

Totals   _____ + _____ + _____ + _____ = _____

(score)

_____ × 5 = _____

Score × 5 = comprehension total

COMMENTS _____

_____

_____

_____

Harcourt Brace School Publishers

Home/School

"*The parent is the child's first teacher and contributes immeasurably to the development of language and literacy.*"

Dr. Eleanor W. Thonis

ANSWERING PARENT QUESTIONS

Dr. Marguerite Cogorno Radencich
University of South Florida, Tampa, Florida

**Impress parents by being prepared to answer questions
that are bound to come up.
You've probably heard several of the following:**

? Is my child getting enough phonics?

Much of the debate surrounding phonics is not about *whether* it is taught, but *how* and *in what sequence.* Look at what is happening in the classroom in addition to phonics instruction. Phonics is one important part— but only a part—of the reading puzzle.

Signs to look for are multiprong approaches that actively engage the child rather than passive activities such as phonics worksheets. Children progress in phonics usage if the teacher provides lots of materials and activities such as the following:

- manipulatives, such as magnetic or cardboard letters, for making words
- invented or temporary spellings, with support for children to move from one developmental level to the next
- interesting books that repeat certain patterns (such as Dr. Seuss's *The Cat in the Hat*)
- language play, such as poems or tongue twisters

? Why is my child allowed to write with invented spelling?

Think of how your child learned to talk. You didn't expect eloquent speech from Day 1. When your child learned to walk, you celebrated every step from sitting up to crawling to standing to taking those first steps. We can recognize similar developmental progressions in writing. There is no fear that a crawling child will stay at that stage forever, yet there is fear that children will not progress beyond invented or temporary spelling. But just as children need to explore their world with blocks, with parents' clothing, and with dirty fingers, they need to explore print. Those who understand the progressions find it fascinating to watch a child first write *I love you* with a heart, and then move to a line of unintelligible print (reflecting knowledge of left-to-right progression), and from there to closer and closer approximations. The more children are able to explore temporary spelling, the faster they move toward conventional spelling.

What can I buy to help my child's reading?

Jim Trelease, author of *The New Read-Aloud Handbook,* talks of the three "*b*'s."

1. First, you should buy <u>b</u>ooks. Children with books close at hand (perhaps in every room of the house) will read more than other children.

2. If you still want to spend more money, you can buy a <u>b</u>ookshelf.

3. And if you still want to spend some more, buy a <u>b</u>ook lamp.

I would extend Trelease's purchases to include magazines, newspapers, magnetic letters, a chalkboard, and endless supplies of paper. The point Trelease and I are making is that these real-life reading and writing materials are much more valuable than commercial programs that promise to cure all maladies. If buying books and related materials sounds too simple, remember that it's the time you spend with your child and with the literacy materials that really make the difference.

What can I do to get my child to read more?

The following tips are tried and true:

- Allow your child to stay up a half hour past bedtime, if that time is spent reading.

- Read to your child every day, even though he or she may also do some reading alone.

- Model reading—don't do all your reading behind a closed door.

- Work with a librarian to help your child select books at the library. Jim Trelease asks parents to compare how often they take their children to the library to how often they take them to the shopping mall!

- Think of reading at gift-giving time. Keeping your child's interests in mind, select storybooks, books of nursery rhymes, books that teach simple concepts, or simple magazines. It's fun for a child to receive a magazine subscription just like grown-ups!

How can I help my child become a better writer?

If you expose your child to many books, you will soon see book language appearing in your child's writing. Hence, reading is one way to make a writer. A second way is practice. Just as piano players get better with practice, so do writers. Leave paper, slate, chalkboard, markers, crayons, and magnetic letters in sight as open invitations for writing and spelling. Celebrate your child's writing by putting it on the refrigerator door and by bragging to anyone who will listen. Search for writing opportunities—a list of children to invite to a birthday party, computer-designed greeting cards, or a journal of drawings and writing for each day of a trip. Don't worry about correctness at this age. The teacher will work on that. Remember that success breeds success. There is nothing more effective for producing writers than helping children see themselves as real authors. 🍎

"Every time you read aloud to your child, you are giving a commercial for reading."
—Jim Trelease

Home, Community, and School Interaction

by Dr. Alma Flor Ada
Director of Doctoral Studies
International Multicultural Program,
University of San Francisco

Children benefit when they experience understanding between the world of their home and community and the world of school. When these two converge, rather than diverge, children have an opportunity to feel whole.

Parents benefit from understanding the goals and purposes of the school, knowing their child's teacher, and being able to share concerns and ideas.

Teachers who bring about interaction between school, home, and community are able to give added meaning to their curriculum and to make their classes more relevant for children. As a first step in creating permanent ties between home, community, and school, teachers can ask themselves some basic questions.

Harcourt Brace School Publishers

For example:

? **What strategies am I developing to ensure the growth of each child's first language (whether I can speak that language or not) as the vehicle for home interaction?**

? **In what ways am I incorporating parents' lives, experiences, and their information and ability to construct knowledge into the school lives of their children?**

? **How can I foster communication at home between parents and children?**

? **What am I doing to use the printed word as a means of validating and celebrating parents?**

? **Are there different ways to encourage parents and children to act as agents of their own liberation?**

As every teacher reflects upon these questions and provides responses based on his or her individual experience, a body of strategies will develop and may be shared within each school among teachers at all levels.

Parent participation can take many forms. This article focuses on participation that takes place on a daily basis and that doesn't necessarily require parents to be physically present in the school. These suggestions may serve as a starting point for sharing among teachers in each educational community.

1. **Encourage children to return home daily with something to share with their parents.** Children might ask a question about a topic they discussed in school that day or share news about a classroom project.

2. **Facilitate interviews of parents by their children.** If the information requested from parents encourages them to revisit their own childhoods, they may in the process develop a greater understanding of their own children. The sharing of childhood memories with their children not only provides a framework for communication but also promotes better parenting.

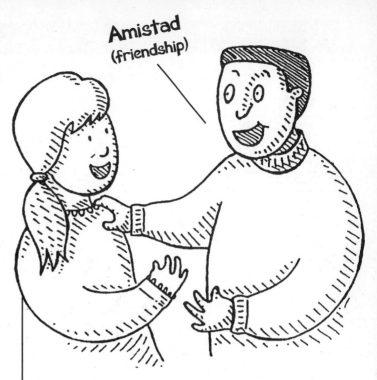

Amistad
(friendship)

3. **Expand whole-language activities outside the classroom.** Just as you ask children to predict the content of a book you are going to read to them—from the title and cover illustration, from names of the characters, or from the first paragraph— you can ask children to invite their parents to offer similar predictions.

4. **Engage children in retelling a story to their parents and then having them ask their parents for a sequel.**

5. **Ask parents to participate in classroom discussions.** For example, if you have discussed the topic of friendship, ask children to interview their parents about childhood friends or about the kinds of games they played or about the ways they resolved conflicts. Children can also learn from their parents how to say *friendship* in the home language and then bring the word back to share with the class.

6. **Children can author books in which they are the protagonists, using information they have obtained from their parents.** For example, they might write about *How I got my name, My autobiography,* or *Something big that happened when I was little.*

Harcourt Brace School Publishers

Use any of these clip-art graphics to create a classroom newsletter to send home.

Insert your school name or newsletter title to head your newsletter.

Personal note to parents

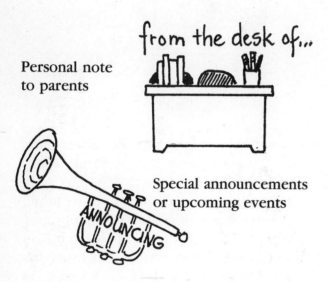

Special announcements or upcoming events

Reminder of upcoming meetings, conferences, or field trips

Classroom projects

Future goals or study themes

List of recommended books for reading

Current events from the classroom, school, or community

Focus on a certain subject area or parent self-help information

Call for volunteers or materials

Student column

Harcourt Brace School Publishers

 News from

 School Bus

Dear Family,
 I'd like to take a
moment to talk about

 SPECIAL ANNOUNCEMENTS

Spotlight on

Something to Try at Home

From Your Child

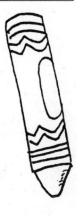

We have been very
busy lately!

BOOK CORNER

Dear Parents,
   As a book is read at home, have your child graph his or her response. Ask your child to write on the line the title of the book and the author's name. Then have your child evaluate the book by coloring a bar on the graph and giving a reason.

Please return this page to school when completed. Thank you.

Book Titles and Authors' Names

1. _____

2. _____

3. _____

4. _____

5. _____

6. _____

Bar Graph

	Would Not Recommend	OK	Good	GREAT!
Book 1				
Book 2				
Book 3				
Book 4				
Book 5				
Book 6				

Parent's signature _____

Harcourt Brace School Publishers

TELEVISION & YOUNG CHILDREN: DEVELOPING CRITICAL THINKING

BY JUDY GIGLIO

Why is television harmful to children? Consider some of the things that children are *not* doing when they are in front of the set:

playing outside
reading
having a conversation
solving problems
asking questions
using their imagination
interacting with the real world
homework or family chores

If most parents are unwilling or unable to limit television in their homes, what can teachers do? They can work with parents to help children develop good viewing habits. Parents *can* teach their children to be selective viewers who use good judgment when tuning in shows.

Description of a TV-Wise Child
- selects programs for good reasons
- spends a limited number of hours viewing TV
- appreciates shows that are well done
- recognizes shows that are poorly done
- knows he or she can ask questions before, during, and after a show

Children will not be able to make smart choices about television all by themselves. They need your help and help from family members. Early in the school year or when you do a family or neighborhood theme, plan to spend some class time talking to children about their television-watching habits. As a follow-up, send home the copying master on page 144. It is designed to

- let parents know you're concerned about children's TV-viewing habits
- make parents aware of their own viewing habits
- offer suggestions for judging the shows children watch
- offer suggestions for home activities that emphasize the positive aspects of television viewing

"Television is the school's primary competitor for children's minds."

Jim Trelease
The Read-Aloud Handbook

Family members, are you setting an example for children of how to view television wisely? Here is a checklist for you.

YES   NO

_____   _____   I often watch the shows my child selects.

_____   _____   My child shares ideas prompted by TV viewing.

_____   _____   My child uses good judgment when selecting shows.

_____   _____   Topics from TV shows often motivate my child to read books for additional information.

_____   _____   I limit the amount of time I view television.

_____   _____   I help my child evaluate the shows he or she watches.

_____   _____   If I object to a show, I explain why to my child.

- If you responded **YES** to every question, you are a **TV-wise parent!**

TV REPORT CARD FOR FAMILY MEMBERS

Watch the shows your children watch. Answer these questions as you watch.

YES   NO

_____   _____   Is this show appropriate for my child's age?

_____   _____   Is the program free of content that might frighten or disturb my child?

_____   _____   Is the program free of violence?

_____   _____   Does the program omit stereotyping of a particular gender, race, or ethnic group?

_____   _____   Does the program offer content that will enhance learning or stimulate my child's imagination?

TV-wise Parents: *Remember, you control the on/off knob! With courage and determination, you can limit television's influence on your children.*

Conferences with parents or guardians are an important opportunity to share information as well as to learn more about the children we are teaching. It is one of the best times to open communication with parents and to make a positive impression. Teachers have different styles of conferencing, and most are perfectly legitimate. Below are ten simple guidelines to help make conferences more successful.

Be prepared.   Have the child's work or portfolio readily accessible. Before the conference, make notes of what you wish to share with the parents. After introductory remarks, begin the conference process. During or after the conference, *immediately* write down what was said. This will help prepare you for the next conference and also document the discussion.

Provide examples.   Parents like to see examples of their child's work. Provide some of the best examples first. Parents also like to see growth and improvement. You will probably want to show an example of the child's writing from early in the school year to compare with a more recent effort.

Discuss strengths first.   Parents need and deserve to hear what their child does well. Let parents know that you focus on strengths. Later you can discuss concerns or opportunities for growth. As a general rule, discuss at least three strengths before addressing any areas of concern.

Avoid jargon.   Speak in a language parents can understand. If you use technical terms, define them briefly. Terms such as metacognition, invented spelling, or K-W-L require an explanation.

Be realistic.   Don't promise something that might not happen during the time a child is in your classroom. If he or she is having trouble, address the issue and talk about *reasonable* expectations. Be optimistic, but realistic. It will save you from parental disappointment later on.

10 GUIDELINES for a SUCCESSFUL PARENT-TEACHER CONFERENCE

by Dr. Timothy Rasinski

Dr. Rasinski is professor of education, Department of Teaching Leadership and Curriculum Studies at Kent State University, Ohio.

Be proactive rather than reactive. Inform parents about what the class will be doing during the year and what the specific areas of focus will be. For example, if you're a first-grade teacher using invented spelling, inform parents of the stages or phases they can expect to see in their child's writing in the coming months. If you suspect that many parents may be unfamiliar with or uncertain about an approach you're taking, prepare them for it in advance rather than waiting to hear from them.

Establish joint responsibility. Use terms such as "what *we* can do," "*our* focus," etc. Talk specifically about how parents can help you and what you intend to do to help them. For example, "If you will continue to read to Brad each night and be sure he sees you reading . . . ."

Establish goals, outcomes, and responsibilities. Tell parents what you plan to do to help their child reach a goal. Then work with them to outline what their responsibilities will be toward that goal. Be sure to discuss the child's responsibilities, too, because you and the family members must be consistent. When children get mixed messages from parents and teachers, they become confused or they may take advantage of the situation.

Invite questions and information. Always ask parents if they have questions about what is occurring in school or why activities are done in a certain way. Encourage parents to share insights into their child's attitudes and behaviors, particularly regarding school. Reassure the parents of children who are having a difficult time personally—a friend has moved away, a pet has died, a family member is ill, etc. Knowledge of these events will be helpful to you.

Promise to be accessible. Invite parents to call or leave a message when they have questions or observations. Give them a time when you like to take calls. Encourage them to be involved in school events and to stay in contact with you. Help parents understand that you want their child's school experience to be a rich and rewarding one just as much as they do.

Harcourt Brace School Publishers

SPECIAL NEEDS OF PARENTS OF YOUNG SECOND-LANGUAGE LEARNERS

BY DR. ELEANOR W. THONIS

Parents and their children are basically the same the world over. Parents love their children and want the best for them. Children love their parents and want to please them. This close relationship between parent and child remains constant among families of *any* language and in *every* culture.

The parent is the child's first teacher and contributes immeasurably to the development of language and literacy. When the child's home language is different from the language of instruction, parents and teachers share special needs in promoting successful learning at home and at school.

At home, parents provide for their children's nutrition, rest, play, safety, and other aspects of their physical development. Parents also help in the acquisition of concepts and in the use of language to express them. While children enjoy listening, speaking, doing, thinking, and talking about everyday experiences at home, they are learning who they are and are beginning to understand the group to which they belong. When children enter school, where many of the people are different from their parents and the language is unfamiliar to them, they encounter a new environment that can be stressful to them. What can parents do to help bridge this gap between home and school? See the chart on the next page.

What Parents Can Do

At Home

- Encourage regular school attendance and make going to school important.

- Display the child's work and express appreciation for the time and effort that have gone into it.

- Assist in the review of homework and call on a neighbor or a friend who can help if needed.

- Promote self-confidence by having faith in the child's skills and talents.

  - Increase responsibility by assigning tasks at home that are within the child's abilities.

  - Keep expectations high.

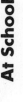

At School

- Go to school to help with activities or to confer with teachers whenever possible.

- Attend classroom and school performances given on special occasions.

- Help in the school library and become acquainted with materials in the language of the home.

- Know the school principal and ask questions about the school routine.

- Bring an interpreter to the school to translate when necessary.

- Allow the child to participate in various school activities.

What can teachers do to make themselves, the school, and the curriculum as accessible as possible for parents of young second-language learners?

- Accept, respect, and enjoy the language of the home.
- Let children write and illustrate their own stories using whatever language they wish.
- Ask children to teach their classmates words of greeting and other amenities in their home language.
- Create a small area in the room where children may go to find books in their home language. At parent conferences, be sure parents know about this area and feel comfortable contributing books, posters, and realia if they wish.

- Invite family members to share their stories, music, art, legends, and folklore. Families might also be asked to share their talents in the classroom, demonstrating needlework, origami, wood carving, and so on.
- Provide literacy activities in the home language with the help of a teacher, parent, or community member who is fluent in both languages.
- Continue to use predictable books for newcomers to English print.
- Help to empower these parents by becoming familiar with organizations and individuals that can assist them in the community, particularly if they are recent arrivals in this country.

Harcourt Brace School Publishers

Professional
Resource
Center

"**L**ike artists, teachers
must be willing to research
and experiment with new
teaching practices."

→ Judy Wallis

TEACHER
by Dr. Judy Wallis

What is *teacher empowerment?* In the broadest sense, it is we teachers taking control over and responsibility for our teaching. Toward this end, we who teach have come to insist that we be treated as professionals—as highly skilled and dedicated practitioners who continually refine our skills and who take our work with the utmost seriousness.

Teaching is sometimes called a practical art, learned best by doing. However, few artists become accomplished without researching and carefully practicing a range of techniques. Artists explore the wide array of potential materials and engage in the rigorous study of other successful artists. An artist's work is enriched by constantly pushing it against the limits set by past work. An artist continually redefines his or her art and, in doing so, finds vital energy and new purpose.

Like artists, teachers must be willing to research and experiment with new teaching practices. We must continually mine the rich resources available for use in our classrooms. We must capitalize on the work of our colleagues and organize time to learn from and with one another.

Brian Cambourne suggests the conditions a child must have to become a successful language learner. When applied to teacher empowerment, these conditions can help us become ever-more-accomplished artists.

Immersion

Just as children learn language from other language users, teachers need other teachers! We thrive when we are nurtured in a community of professionals eager to learn. Being with people committed to a lifetime of learning ensures a dynamic and creative environment for students and teachers.

Demonstration

Just as young children learn through demonstrations, teachers learn by observing skilled colleagues. The opportunity to watch another teacher often ends with student teaching. Since most teachers have not experienced programs based upon current philosophy, we need to see others in order to envision these new ideas.

Engagement

Young learners quickly participate in the demonstrations that occur all around them. They become engaged because they see potential and purpose in what others do. As teachers, we must see potential and purpose in our teaching. Growth occurs because we believe we can become master teachers. Our growth, like the artist's growth, is dependent on our willingness to explore.

Harcourt Brace School Publishers

EMPOWERMENT

Expectation

Children sense that they are capable of learning from those around them. Teachers need to develop that same assurance. Through goal setting, discussion, and coaching one another, we refine our teaching and learn to consider future possibilities.

Approximation

As teachers, we often adopt a "get-it-right-the-first-time" attitude. Imagine what new learning would not have occurred if we had assumed that philosophy as children! Trying new ideas and methods in our classrooms will often begin with awkward first attempts. However, recognizing and using the freedom to approximate will yield maximum benefits for ourselves and our students.

Response

Teachers respond to students constantly: we praise them, we celebrate their successes, we accept their first attempts, we encourage and extend them. Shouldn't we do those same things for ourselves and our colleagues? Reflecting with other teachers, celebrating successes, and encouraging one another promotes learning and empowers people.

Sure Steps to Empowerment

- Watch other teachers teach; talk with them about what you noticed.
- Form a study group of teachers, and read and discuss professional books or articles.
- Take risks! Try new materials or strategies.
- Attend workshops and professional meetings.
- Set professional goals, and monitor your progress toward achieving them.
- Believe in yourself!

Professional Bookshelf

Adams, M.J. (1994). *Beginning to Read: Thinking and Learning About Print.* Cambridge, MA: MIT Press.

Allington, R.L. & Cunningham, P.M. (1995). *Schools That Work: All Children, Readers & Writers.* New York: HarperCollins.

Anderson, R., et al. (Eds.). (1985). *Becoming a Nation of Readers: The Report of the Commission on Reading.* Champaign, IL: Center for the Study of Reading.

Asher, J. (1988). *Learning Another Language Through Actions.* Los Gatos, CA: Sky Oaks Productions.

Bandy, E.B. (1991). Helping teachers to understand and improve their students' speech patterns. *Black Communications: Breaking Down the Barriers.* African American Images.

Banks, J.A., & Banks, C.M. (Eds.). (1989). *Multicultural Education: Issues and Perspectives.* Boston: Allyn and Bacon.

Barron, M. (1990). *I Learn to Read and Write the Way I Learn to Talk.* Katonah, NY: Owen.

Baskwill, J. (1988). Themestorming. *Teaching K–8,* 19(1), 80–82.

Bear, D. (1992). The Prosody of Oral Reading and Stages of Word Knowledge. In S. Templeton & D. Bear (Eds.) *Development of Orthographic Knowledge: The Foundations of Literacy: A Memorial Festschrift for Edmund H. Henderson.* Hillsdale, NJ: Lawrence Erlbaum.

Bear, D.R., Invernizzi, M., & Templeton, S. (1995). *Words Their Way: Word Study for Phonics, Vocabulary, and Spelling.* Englewood Cliffs, NJ: Prentice Hall.

Berghoff, B., & Egawa, K. (1991). No more "rocks": Grouping to give students control of their learning. *The Reading Teacher,* 44(8), 536–541.

Bloom, B.S. (Ed.). (1985). *Developing Talent in Young People.* New York: Ballantine Books.

Book Links. (Bimonthly). Chicago, IL: American Library Association.

Bredekamp, S. (Ed.). (1987). *Developmentally Appropriate Practice in Early Childhood Programs Serving Children from Birth Through Age 8.* Washington, DC: NAEYC.

Brown, H., & Mathie, V. (1990). *Inside Whole Language: A Classroom View.* Portsmouth, NH: Heinemann.

Brown, R. (1977). Introduction to Snow and Ferguson. In C. Snow and C. Ferguson (Eds.) *Talking to Children.* New York: Cambridge University Press. 1–27.

Butler, A., & Turbill, J. (1987). *Towards a Reading-Writing Classroom.* Portsmouth, NH: Heinemann.

Caine, R.N., & Caine, G. (1991). *Making Connections: Teaching and the Human Brain.* Alexandria, VA: Association for Supervision and Curriculum Development.

Calkins, L.M. (1986). *The Art of Teaching Writing.* Portsmouth, NH: Heinemann.

Calkins, L.M. (1991). *Living Between the Lines.* Portsmouth, NH: Heinemann.

Cambourne, B. (1988). *The Whole Story: National Learning and the Acquisition of Literacy in the Classroom.* Auckland, New Zealand: Ashton, Scholastic.

Clay, M. (1993). *An Observation Survey: Of Early Literacy Achievement.* Portsmouth, NH: Heinemann.

Clay, M. (1993). *Reading Recovery: A Guidebook for Teachers in Training.* Portsmouth, NH: Heinemann.

Clymer, T. (1963). The utility of phonic generalizations in the primary grades. *The Reading Teacher,* 16(4), 252–258.

Crafton, L. (1994). *Challenges of Holistic Teaching: Answering the Tough Questions.* Norwood, MA: Christopher-Gordon.

Cullinan, B.E. (Ed.). (1992). *Invitation to Read: More Children's Literature in the Reading Program.* Newark, DE: International Reading Association.

Cullinan, B.E., & Galda, L. (1994). *Literature and the Child.* Third ed. Fort Worth, TX: Harcourt Brace.

Cunningham, P.M. (1990). *Phonics They Use.* New York: HarperCollins.

Cunningham, P.M., & Cunningham, J.W. (1992). Making words: Enhancing the invented spelling-decoding connection. *The Reading Teacher,* 46(2), 106–115.

Dakos, K. (1990). *If You're Not Here, Please Raise Your Hand: Poems About School.* New York: Macmillan.

DiYanni, R. (1985). *Connections: Writing, Reading, and Thinking.* Portsmouth, NH: Heinemann.

Dole, J.A., et al. (1991). Moving from the old to the new: Research on reading comprehension instruction. *Review of Educational Research,* 61(2), 239–264.

Dyson, A.H. (1982). Reading, writing, and language: Young children solving the written language puzzle. *Language Arts,* 59(8), 829–839.

Elkind, D. (1988). *The Hurried Child.* Reading, MA: Addison Wesley.

Fagan, W.T. (1989). Empowered students; empowered teachers. *The Reading Teacher,* 42(8), 572–578.

Farr, R. (1990). Setting directions for language arts portfolios. *Educational Leadership,* 48(3), 103.

Farr, R. (1992). Putting it all together. *The Reading Teacher,* 46(1), 26–37.

Flood, J., & Lapp, D. (1989). Reporting reading progress: A comparison portfolio for parents. *The Reading Teacher,* 42(7), 508–514.

Flores, B., Tefft Cousin, P., & Diaz, E. (1991). Transforming deficit myths about learning, language, and culture. *Language Arts,* 68(5), 369–379.

Fogarty, R. (1991). Ten ways to integrate curriculum. *Educational Leadership,* 49(2), 61–65.

Fox, Barbara J. (1996). *Strategies for Word Identification: Phonics from a New Perspective.* Englewood Cliffs, NJ: Macmillan.

Fredericks, A., Meinbach, A.M., & Rothlein, L. (1992). *Thematic Units: An Integrated Approach to Teaching Science and Social Studies.* New York: HarperCollins.

Freppom, P., & Dahl, K. (1991). Learning about phonics in a whole-language classroom. *Language Arts,* 68(3), 190–197.

Gardner, H. (1985). *Frames of Mind: The Theory of Multiple Intelligences.* New York: Basic Books.

Garrett, J. (1993). Faraway wisdom: Three nominees for the 1992 Andersen prize. *The Reading Teacher,* 46(4), 310–314.

Gentry, J.R. (1989). *Spel Is a Four-Letter Word.* Portsmouth, NH: Heinemann.

Goodman, Y.M. (1989). Evaluation of Students. In K.S. Goodman, Y.M. Goodman, and W. Hood (Eds.) *The Whole Language Evaluation Book.* Portsmouth, NH: Heinemann.

Goodman, Y.M. (Ed.). (1990). *How Children Construct Literacy.* Newark, DE: International Reading Association.

Graves, D. (1989). *Writing: Teachers and Children at Work.* Portsmouth, NH: Heinemann.

Gunning, T.G. (1995). Word building: A strategic approach to the teaching of phonics. *The Reading Teacher,* 48(6), 484-488.

Harp, B. (1989). How are we using what we know about literacy processes in the content areas? *The Reading Teacher,* 42(7), 726–727.

Harste, J., & Short, K.G., with Burke, C. (1988). *Creating Classrooms for Authors: The Reading-Writing Connection.* Portsmouth, NH: Heinemann.

Harwayne, S. (1993). *Lasting Impressions: Weaving Literature into the Writing Workshop.* Portsmouth, NH: Heinemann.

Henderson, A. (1988). Parents are a school's best friend. *Phi Delta Kappan,* 70(2), 148–153.

Hilliard, A.G., III. (1991). Do we have the will to educate all children? *Educational Leadership,* 49(1), 31–36.

Hilliard, A.G., III. (1991). Why we must pluralize the curriculum. *Educational Leadership,* 49(4), 12–15.

Hopkins, L.B. (1987). *Pass the Poetry, Please!* New York: HarperCollins.

Hoyt, L. (1992). Many ways of knowing: Using drama, oral interactions, and the visual arts to enhance reading comprehension. *The Reading Teacher,* 45(8), 580–584.

Johns, J.L. (1991). Helping readers at risk: Beyond whole language, whole word, and phonics. *International Journal of Reading, Writing, and Learning Disabilities,* 7(1), 59–67.

Johnson, D.W., Johnson, R.T., & Holubec, E.J. (1994). *The New Circles of Learning: Cooperation in the Classroom and School.* Alexandria, VA: Association for Supervision and Curriculum Development.

Kasten, W.C., & Clarke, B.K. (1993). *The Multi-age Classroom—A Family of Learners.* Katonah, NY: Owen.

Kidder, T. (1989). *Among Schoolchildren.* Boston: Houghton Mifflin.

Kutiper, K., & Pope, C. (1988). Using magazines in the English classroom. *English Journal,* 7(8), 66–68.

Langer, J. (Ed.). (1992). *Literature Instruction: A Focus on Student Response.* Urbana, IL: National Council of Teachers of English.

Larrick, N. (1991). *Let's Do a Poem: Introducing Poetry to Children.* New York: Delacorte.

Leonhardt, M. (1993). *Parents Who Love Reading, Kids Who Don't: What Happened and What to Do.* New York: Crown.

Lindgren, M. (1991). *The Multicolored Mirror: Cultural Substance in Literature for Children and Young Adults.* Fort Atkinson, WI: Highsmith Press.

McCarthy, B. (1985). What 4Mat training teaches us about staff development. *Educational Leadership,* 42(7), 61–68.

Michel, P. (1994). *The Child's View of Reading: Understandings for Teachers and Parents.* Boston: Allyn and Bacon.

Mills, H., O'Keefe, T., & Stephens, D. (1992). *Looking Closely: Exploring the Role of Phonics in One Whole Language Classroom.* Urbana, IL: National Council of Teachers of English.

Mooney, M. (1991). *Developing Life-Long Readers.* New York: Richard C. Owens.

Newkirk, T. (1989). *More Than Stories: The Range of Children's Writing.* Portsmouth, NH: Heinemann.

Norton, D.E. (1990). Teaching multicultural literature in the reading curriculum. *The Reading Teacher,* 44(1), 28–40.

Ogle, D. (1986). K-W-L: A teaching model that develops active reading of expository text. *The Reading Teacher,* 39(7), 564–570.

Pearce, M. (1995). Where should phonics fit in your reading toolbox? *Instructor,* 104(8), 55-59.

Pellowski, A. (1968). *The World of Children's Literature.* New York: R.R. Bowker.

Pellowski, A. (1990). *The World of Storytelling.* Second ed. New York: H.W. Wilson.

Peterson, R., & Eeds, M. (1990). *Grand Conversations: Literature Groups in Action.* Richmond Hill, Ontario: Scholastic TAB.

Pikulski, J. (1994). Preventing reading failure: A review of five effective programs. *Reading Teacher,* 48, 30-39.

Preece, A., & Cowden, D. (1993). *Young Writers in the Making.* Portsmouth, NH: Heinemann.

Radencich, M.C., & McKay, L.J. (1995). *Flexible Grouping for Literacy in the Elementary Grades.* Boston: Allyn & Bacon.

Rasinski, T. (1989). Reading and the empowerment of parents. *The Reading Teacher,* 43(3), 226–231.

Rasinski, T. (1994). *Parents, Teachers, and Literacy Learning.* Fort Worth, TX: Harcourt Brace.

Rasinski, T., & Fredericks, A. (1989–1991). "Working with Parents" column. *The Reading Teacher,* 43 and 44.

Read, C. (1975). *Children's Categorization of Speech Sounds in English.* Urbana, IL: National Council of Teachers of English.

Reimer, B.L., & Warshow, L. (1989). Questions we ask of ourselves and our students. *The Reading Teacher,* 42(8), 596–606.

Reutzel, D.R., & Fawson, P. (1990). Travelling tales: Connecting parents and children through writing. *The Reading Teacher,* 44(3), 222–227.

Rigg, P., & Allen, V.G. (1989). *When They Don't All Speak English.* Urbana, IL: National Council of Teachers of English.

Routman, R. (1991). *Invitations: Changing as Teachers and Learners K–12.* Portsmouth, NH: Heinemann.

Royer, J.M., & Carlo, M.S. (1991). Transfer of comprehension skills from native to second language. *Journal of Reading,* 34(6), 450–455.

Samuels, S.J. (1988). Decoding and automaticity: Helping poor readers become automatic at word recognition. *The Reading Teacher,* 41(8), 756–760.

Short, K., & Pierce, K. (1990). *Talking About Books: Creating Literate Communities.* Portsmouth, NH: Heinemann.

Spiegel, D. (1995). A comparison of traditional remedial programs and Reading Recovery: Guidelines for success for all programs. *Reading Teacher,* 49(2), 86-95.

Stahl, S.A., et al. (1990). *Beginning to Read: Thinking and Learning About Print—A Summary.* Champaign, IL: Center for the Study of Reading.

Strickland, D. (1995). Reinventing our literacy programs: Books, basics, balance. *The Reading Teacher,* 48(4), 294-302.

Strickland, D., & Feely, J. (1987). *Using Computers in the Teaching of Reading.* New York: Teachers College Press.

Strickland, D., & Morrow, L. (1989). Creating curriculum: An emergent literacy perspective. *The Reading Teacher,* 42(9), 722–723.

Strickland, D., & Morrow, L. (Eds.). (1989). *Emerging Literacy: Young Children Learn to Read and Write.* Newark, DE: International Reading Association.

Swanson, M. (1991). *At-Risk Students in Elementary Education.* Springfield, IL: Charles C. Thomas.

Taylor, D. (1983). *Family Literacy.* Portsmouth, NH: Heinemann.

Teale, W.H., & Sulzby, E. (Eds.). (1986). *Emerging Literacy: Writing and Reading.* Norwood, NJ: Ablex.

Trachtenburg, P. (1990). Using children's literature to enhance phonics instruction. *The Reading Teacher,* 43(9), 648-654.

Trachtenburg, P., & Ferruggia, A. (1989). Big books from little voices: Reaching high-risk beginning readers. *The Reading Teacher,* 42(4), 284–289.

Trelease, J. (1995). *The Read-Aloud Handbook.* New York: Viking.

Tunnell, M.O., & Jacobs, J.S. (1989). Using "real" books: Research findings on literature-based reading instruction. *The Reading Teacher,* 42(7), 470–477.

The WEB: Wonderfully Exciting Books. (quarterly). Columbus, OH: Ohio State University.

Wepner, S.B., & Seminoff, N.E. (1994). Saving endangered species: Using technology to teach thematically. *The Computing Teacher,* 22(1), 34-37.

Wilde, S. (1992). *You Kan Red This!* Portsmouth, NH: Heinemann.

Yokota, J. (1993). Issues in selecting multicultural children's literature. *Language Arts,* 70(3), 156–167.

Yopp, H.K. (1992). Developing phonemic awareness in young children. *The Reading Teacher,* 45(9), 696-703.

Yopp, H.K. (1995). Read-aloud books for developing phonemic awareness: An annotated bibliography. *The Reading Teacher,* 48, 538-542.

Yopp, H.K. (1995). A test for assessing phonemic awareness in young children. *The Reading Teacher,* 49, 20-29.

SOFTWARE RESOURCES

Annotated Bibliography of Reading/Language Arts Technology. (1995). Harcourt Brace.

Flexible grouping—A multimedia workshop. Needham, MA: Silver Burdett Ginn.

The Latest & Best of the Educational Software Selector (TESS). (1994). New York: Educational Products Information Exchange Institute (Teachers College Press).

Microcomputer Index. (Updated quarterly, bound into annual volumes. Also available as an on-line database). Mountain View, CA: Database Services.

Neill, S.B., & Neill, G.W. *Only the Best: Annual Guide to the Highest-Rated Education Software—Multimedia for Preschool–Grade 12.* Education News Service.

Software Reviews on File. (Monthly binders). New York: Facts on File.

Educational Software Packages
Bailey's Book House by Edmark
Explore-A-Science Series by William K. Bradford
KidWorks 2 by Davidson & Associates
Learn About Series by Wings for Learning/Sunburst
Living Books by Brøderbund
Make-A-Book by Teacher Support Software
My First Encyclopedia by Knowledge Adventure
Random House Kid's Encyclopedia by Knowledge Adventure
Reader Rabbit's Interactive Reading Journey by The Learning Company
Zoo Keeper by Davidson & Associates

VIDEO RESOURCES

Making Meaning: Integrated Language Arts Series. (1992). Association for Supervision and Curriculum Development in cooperation with the International Reading Association.

Teaching Reading: Strategies from Successful Classrooms. (1991). Center for the Study of Reading.

Harcourt Brace School Publishers

GLOSSARY OF PROFESSIONAL TERMS

ASSESSMENT   The process of observing, recording, and otherwise documenting work that children do and how they do it and using these findings as a basis for a variety of educational decisions that affect the child. (from NAEYC)

AUDITORY ACTIVITY   An activity in which children identify and differentiate sounds, rhyming words, and/or other word patterns.

AUTHOR'S CHAIR   A special chair in which a student author sits to read his/her writing for response from a group or from the class.

AUTOMATICITY   A state of mental functioning producing a seemingly instantaneous understanding of the task.

BIG BOOK   An enlarged book that children can see from a distance and can read in a group; re-creates the lap method of teaching reading in a school setting, since children can see the words as they hear them read aloud.

BRAINSTORMING   Expressing ideas without stopping to evaluate them; searching for ideas or solutions through group discussion; a prewriting strategy.

CHORAL READING   Reading verse or other patterned language in groups, sometimes by alternating lines or passages.

COMMUNITY OF READERS   A classroom in which children have an integral part in defining reading roles, routines, and rules and have a sense that reading is a worthwhile, meaningful experience that should be shared.

CONSTRUCTIVISM   The theory that meaningful learning is not passive but is inquiry-based and student-centered.

CONTEXTUAL CLUES   Meaning clues provided by the words surrounding the word to be decoded.

CONVENTIONAL WRITING   Writing that exhibits the conventions of English, including sentence structure, spelling, punctuation, capitalization, and grammar.

COOPERATIVE LEARNING   Working in pairs or small groups to accomplish goals and generate products interdependently; children may be assigned specific roles such as Reader, Recorder, and Reporter.

CREATIVE DRAMATICS   Informally acting out a story or a poem.

CREATIVE THINKING   Generating and expressing thoughts imaginatively, uniquely, or poetically, through relational patterns of language and thought.

CRITICAL THINKING   Making judgments about the validity, quality, and accuracy of ideas or text; judging the actions and traits of a character; logical analysis and judgment of worth, based on sound criteria.

CROSS-CHECKING   Procedure in which readers take advantage of multiple cueing systems (phonics, syntax, context, and illustrations) to determine and confirm a word's pronunciation.

DECODING   Turning print into language; determining letter-sound correspondences; constructing meaning from the graphic symbols of language.

DEVELOPMENTALLY APPROPRIATE PRACTICE   Matching a curriculum and an environment to a particular age group's developmental level.

DIALOGUING   Talking in pairs or small groups; carrying on a written or spoken dialogue; specifically, ongoing written conversation between a teacher and a child.

ECHO READING   A form of reading in which students repeat phrases after the teacher.

EMERGENT LITERACY   The reading and writing behaviors of young children that precede and develop into conventional literacy.

EMPOWERMENT   The proactive stance teachers must assume if they are to have a voice in creating a new kind of educational community.

ENCODING   Transcribing spoken language into written symbols.

FLEXIBLE GROUPING   Temporary grouping that varies according to instructional goals and students' needs and interests; includes whole groups, teacher-facilitated small groups, cooperative groups, pairs, and individuals.

GRAPHIC ORGANIZER   A visual representation that aids meaning; a vehicle for organizing ideas to show relationships among them; webs, charts, and diagrams.

GRAPHO-PHONEMIC   A term that relates to print-sound relationships; one part of a cueing system readers use to make sense of text. (from Ken Goodman)

INFORMAL ASSESSMENT   Observation of children's progress to diagnose children's needs; a sampling of ability or performance, including portfolios in which representative samples of children's work are gathered over time.

INTEGRATED CURRICULUM   Teaching social studies, science, math, language arts, and other content areas as related parts of a whole.

INTELLIGENCE   The ability to solve problems, or to fashion products that are valued in one or more cultural or community settings. (from Howard Gardner)

INVENTED OR TEMPORARY SPELLING   The spelling of emergent readers and writers that follows a developmental progression which moves from drawing and scribbling to gradually closer approximations of words.

KID WATCHING   The process of monitoring children's ongoing development through daily activities that are integral to instruction.

KINESTHETIC ACTIVITY   An activity involving physical movement or touch, such as tracing sandpaper letters, jumping, or walking; an activity in which learning is promoted through movement.

K-W-L   A learning strategy for reading nonfiction, consisting of listing what you *know*, what you *want* to know, and what you have *learned*.

LEARNING STYLES   Ways in which we learn: visual, auditory, and kinesthetic are the three most frequently used in school.

LITERATURE-BASED   Characterized by the use of high-quality stories, poems, plays, and nonfiction to teach reading, writing, listening, and speaking.

METACOGNITION   A level of thinking that involves the examination of one's own state of knowledge; awareness of thinking and learning processes; "thinking about thinking."

MINILESSON   A brief instructional session, provided when a teacher diagnoses a need, in which concepts, skills, or strategies are introduced in a meaningful context through student-teacher interaction.

MODELING   A demonstration of behaviors for novices to imitate; "thinking aloud" to make explicit or public what one does or thinks about while reading, writing, listening, or speaking.

Harcourt Brace School Publishers

MULTI-AGE Classrooms (sometimes called "nongraded") in which children of several ages are taught together.

MULTICULTURALISM The inclusion, integration, and appreciation of literature, concepts, art, contributions, and values of diverse cultural groups.

PHONEMIC AWARENESS The understanding that spoken language is composed of a series of separate sounds; the ability to segment language into phonemes.

PHONICS The science of matching speech sounds to printed letters in reading and spelling.

PORTFOLIO ASSESSMENT Evaluation based on the regular collection of samples of children's work over a period of time.

PREDICTABLE TEXT Highly patterned, rhythmic, structured text in which a sentence pattern, a sound, or a rhyme is repeated.

PREVIEWING AND PREDICTING A pre-reading strategy that involves looking over a text to infer what it might be about and how it should be read.

READER RESPONSE The construction of meaning from text; active and personal participation in reading and responding.

READERS THEATRE A literature response activity in which children translate a narrative or poem into a script and read it aloud; a simply staged performance that requires little preparation.

SCAFFOLDING Supporting a novice learner by modeling dialogue and responses and then gradually withdrawing support as a learner becomes increasingly independent.

SHARED READING The group reading of a book—generally a big book—while a teacher or child points to the words.

SHARED WRITING An interactive group-writing process in which teachers and children work together to compose or record meaningful messages and stories.

STORY THEATER Groups of students each reading parts of a selection while other students pantomime the action.

STRATEGY A systematic plan for achieving a specific goal or result; an approach to learning that gives children methods for mastering tasks and gaining skills.

SYNTACTIC CLUES Grammatical clues (for decoding a word) provided by the position the word holds within the sentence.

THEME A central or dominating idea around which reading materials, concepts, and instruction can be organized; a message or idea that dominates a work of literature or art.

VIEWING Learning from and evaluating visual media such as illustrations, photographs, videos, and TV.

VISUAL ACTIVITY An activity that involves discrimination between colors, shapes, and other visual stimuli.

WHOLE LANGUAGE An instructional approach based on the beliefs that learning is a social experience and that children learn from complete texts, high-quality literature, integrated instruction, and ongoing experimentation with language.

WRITER'S WORKSHOP A block of time devoted to writing; can include minilessons and the writing process; a session that provides time to write, ownership of written products, and time to share them.

WRITING PROCESS A framework for writing in which children use some or all of the following steps: prewriting, drafting, responding and revising, proofreading, and publishing; an approach to writing that allows children to shape and reshape their language over a period of time.

F

Facilitator, teacher as, 6, 8–10, 63, 64–66, 68–72, 84–85, 118–119, 120–121
Family involvement, 32–33, 89, 90, 97, 109, 113, 138–139
  parent conferences, 136–137, 145–146
  parents of second-language learners, 147–148
  television and, 143–144
Folktales, 30–31, 60, 113
Functional print, 11–13, 87, 114

G

Gardner, Howard, 94
Genre, 13, 26–27, 28–29, 30–31, 41–44, 69, 85, 112
Gifted and talented children, 115–116
Graphic organizers
  chart, 14–16, 53, 62–63, 87, 115
  graph, 16
  K-W-L, 16, 62, 71, 115
  story map, 34, 96, 114
  web, 14, 24, 63
Group retelling, 41–44, 53
Grouping, 68, 73–75, 80–83, 87
  See also Classroom management.

H

Handwriting, 61
Heterogeneous grouping, 68, 80–83

I

Illustrations, story, 13
Individual needs.
  See Grouping; Learning styles.
Integrated curriculum, 29, 68–72, 73–75, 114
  art, 12, 116
  language arts, 13, 41–44, 64–66, 114, 115–116
  math, 14–16, 116
  multicultural infusion, 30–31, 32–33, 99–102
  music, 12, 116
  reading strategies, 13, 21, 34–35
  science, 15
  spelling, 57–59
  vocabulary, 36–37
  writing. *See* Writing.
  See also Learning centers; Literature.
Interpretive reading, 44, 112–114
Intervention, early, 105–107
Invented spelling, 49, 55, 58–59, 125, 136, 146
IQ tests, 95

J

Journals, 88–90
  class, 14, 64, 82, 90
  dialogue, 82, 90
  personal, 16, 56, 88–90
  response, 34, 56, 82, 114

K

Kid watching.
  See Assessment.
K-W-L.
  See Graphic organizers.

L

Language acquisition.
  See Students Acquiring English.
Language arts.
  See Integrated curriculum.
Language experience, 15, 49, 50, 51–53, 64–66, 97–99, 110
Learning centers, 9, 10, 12–13, 73–75, 81–82, 87
Learning styles, 32, 41–44, 94–96
Letter names, 58–59
Library, classroom.
  See Reading center.
Limited English Proficiency.
  See Students Acquiring English.
Listening, 41–44, 82, 86–87, 97–98, 109, 148
Literary elements, 13, 42–44
Literature
  appreciation for, 26–27
  integrating the curriculum with, 26–29, 39, 60–61, 64–66, 68–72, 115–116
  listening to, 21–25, 40–44, 64–66, 112–113, 148
  multicultural, 30–31, 32–33, 148
  poetry, 26–29, 33, 112
  response to. *See* Reader response.
  vocabulary and, 36–37
  writing and, 60–61, 64–66, 73–75, 82, 116
Literature-based reading approach, 13, 26–29, 30–31, 36–37, 47–49, 64–66, 68–72, 91–92, 112–114, 116

M

McCarthy, Bernice, 94, 95
Math activities, 14–16, 116
Meeting individual needs
  gifted and talented, 24, 115–116
  learning styles, 32, 62–63, 94–96, 115–116
  low-achieving students, 24, 83, 92, 108–110
  minilessons for, 60, 61, 75, 84–85
  multiple intelligences, 94–96, 115–116
  reluctant readers and writers, 24, 62–63, 92, 111–112

second-language support, 30–31, 32–33, 97–98, 99–102, 147–148
  strategies for, 27, 30–31, 32–33, 62–63, 80–83, 91–92, 94–96, 97–99, 147–148
  See also Developmentally appropriate practice.
Metacognition, 94–96
Minilessons, 38, 60, 61, 75, 84–85
Modeling, 21, 34–35, 38, 48, 61, 84–85, 91, 108, 115
Multiculturalism, 30–31, 32–33, 148
Multiple intelligences, 94–96
Music activities, 12, 33, 74, 116

N

Newsletters, home/school, 140, 141
Nursery rhymes, 18–20, 28–29, 64, 112

O

Observation.
  See Assessment.
Oral language.
  See Listening; Speaking.
Oral reading, 13, 33, 34–35, 41–42, 57–59, 64, 82, 104, 110, 112
  See also Choral reading; Shared reading.

P

Pacing instruction, 91–92
Parent involvement.
  See Family involvement.
Participation stories, 42, 112
Personal response to literature.
  See Reader response.
Phonemic awareness, 18–20
Phonics, 45–50
  in context, 57, 110
  as a cueing system, 57, 103
  generalizations, 84
  instruction in, 49–50, 84, 136–137
  invented spelling, 55, 57–59, 84, 136
  letter names and, 58–59, 84
  phonemic awareness and, 18–20
  rules in, 84
  spelling and, 55–56, 57–59, 84
  word families, 59, 110
Poetry, 26–27, 28–29, 33, 48, 53, 58, 112
Portfolios, 70, 75, 120–121
  See also Assessment.
Prediction, 23, 109
Prewriting activities, 53, 61, 62–63
Print, conventions of, 23, 54–56, 60–61, 84–85, 124–125
Print-rich environment, 6, 11–13, 14–16, 47, 49, 56, 64–66, 73–75, 111, 148
Process writing, 51–53, 60–61, 62–63
Projects, 10, 64–66, 74, 75
Publishing, 64–66

Harcourt Brace School Publishers